THE KISTE AND OGAN SOCIAL CHANGE

SERIES IN ANTHROPOLOGY

Editors

ROBERT C. KISTE   EUGENE OGAN

University of Minnesota

Bob Tonkinson was born and raised in Perth, Western
Australia, and received his B.A. and M.A. in social anthropology from the University of Western Australia. In
addition to fieldwork in Australia, he has done field
research in Melanesia (New Hebrides) on a relocation
project directed by Homer Barnett (University of Oregon).
Following the award of a Ph.D. in anthropology from the
University of British Columbia in 1972, Dr. Tonkinson
returned to the University of Oregon, where he had
taught for a year before moving to Canada, and has a
current appointment as assistant professor of anthropology.
He is also continuing his research work in Australia
supported by the Australian National University and the
Australian Institute of Aboriginal Studies. Dr. Tonkinson's
subject interests are social organization, religion, social
change, and film; his area interests are Aboriginal
Australia and Oceania.

Cummings Publishing Company

Aboriginal Victors of the Desert Crusade

ROBERT TONKINSON

University of Oregon

Menlo Park, California

To the memory of my parents,

John and Ellen Tonkinson

Cummings Publishing Company, Inc.
2727 Sand Hill Road
Menlo Park, California 94025

Foreword

The Jigalong Mob: Aboriginal Victors of the Desert Crusade is an important contribution to a subfield belatedly emerging within anthropology: the anthropology of colonialism. Members of the Jigalong "Mob," like other Australian Aborigines, American Indians, Pacific Islanders, and Africans before independence, have seen their traditional home invaded by aliens who possess a more developed technology and a ruthless sense of their own superiority. But unlike many others, including their brothers elsewhere on the continent, these Aborigines had not — at the time they offered the anthropologist their cooperation — succumbed to the despair, inferiority feelings, and anomie so painfully familiar among colonized peoples.

A series of fringe settlements has developed in the Western Desert of Australia in which Aborigines from several different linguistic groups have integrated with varying degrees of success. Dr. Tonkinson has focused on a settlement based in the 1960s on a Protestant mission station at Jigalong, the inhabitants of which have become known among other Aborigines for their success in maintaining their "Law" — that is, their traditional religion and values and, thereby, their ethnic identity and pride.

The author provides a wealth of material to explain the persistence of Aboriginal values and ethnic pride at Jigalong. One particularly valuable aspect of his book is the attention paid to the subculture of the white missionaries, for all too often colonialist culture is given scant treatment by the anthropologist. Further, this study provides ready refutation of any crude materialist notion that religion is simply epiphenomenal to social and economic conditions, for it is precisely in the Aboriginal religious system that Dr. Tonkinson finds the greatest strength to resist colonial pressures.

This case study adds a new dimension to our series on social and cultural change. Based on the author's original field research, his book is concerned with people who have long fascinated laymen and anthropologists alike. The former have regarded Aborigines as uniquely "primitive"; the latter have found the particular combination of extremely simple technology and elaborate, integrated social and religious systems which characterizes Aboriginal culture a rewarding subject for continued research.

Although the residents of Jigalong differ in many ways from the African and Mexican town dwellers and the snowmobile-riding Lapps who are the subjects of earlier books in this series, these Aborigines, too, face the problem of adapting to modifications in their traditional environment. In the case of the Jigalong Mob, this problem takes the form of invasion by white men, some of whom — the missionaries — have as their avowed purpose the destruction of traditional Aboriginal culture.

Living in what Europeans regard as a most inhospitable setting, Aborigines of the Western Desert had nonetheless been able to achieve a successful adaptation as hunters and gatherers, one which permitted the rich elaboration of religious life characteristic of indigenous Australia. As Dr. Tonkinson makes clear, the arid and forbidding environment delayed European penetration of this part of the continent, and protected the Western Desert Aborigines from being displaced and overwhelmed by white men when the invaders finally appeared. Unlike their brothers to the east, south, and southwest, these Aborigines had the chance to exercise some control over their degree of contact with European civilization.

Later works in this series, including the editors' own books on Bikini and Bougainville respectively, will present other studies of colonial situations. In the meantime, we are fortunate to have the present unique contribution to our knowledge of the anthropology of colonialism, of social change, and of Aboriginal society.

University of Minnesota ROBERT C. KISTE
Minneapolis, Minnesota EUGENE OGAN
Series Editors

Acknowledgments

In the period since 1963 I have been indebted to many people and several organizations whose assistance I have greatly appreciated. Financial aid from the University of Western Australia, Australian Universities Commission, Australian Institute of Aboriginal Studies, and the University of British Columbia helped make the various field trips possible. Officials in the Western Australian Native Welfare Department cooperated willingly at all stages of research and enabled me to accompany several desert patrols. Many members of the Anthropology Department at the University of Western Australia gave me valuable advice and support during the early fieldwork periods, but I am particularly indebted to Ron and Catherine Berndt, D'Arcy Ryan, and Thyra Robertson. At the University of British Columbia, my thesis supervisor Ken Burridge, and committee members Cyril Belshaw, Mike Egan, Mike Kew, and Pierre Maranda helped me to interpret my Aboriginal data.

For their many helpful comments on an earlier draft of this book, I thank my wife Myrna, Dick and Betsy Gould, Bob Kiste, Eugene Ogan, Al Schütz, Craig Severance, and Harry Wolcott.

To Trevor and Peggy Levien and David and Gloria Goold, all formerly of Jigalong, I extend my grateful thanks for their hospitality and friendship; thank you too, Joe Criddle and Charlie Snell, for your cold beer and good yarns.

Finally, I offer my heartfelt thanks to the people whose friendship and cooperation made my work possible: the Aborigines, who accepted my presence with patience and good humor and kindly allowed me to witness many objects and activities normally kept secret from outsiders. I hope that this book in some way justifies the confidence they had in me as a concerned friend.

Eugene, Oregon ROBERT TONKINSON

Contents

Illustrations

PHOTOGRAPHS

MAPS

CHAPTER ONE

Introduction

Since their existence was first reported to Europe over 300 years ago, the Australian Aborigines have been held up to the Western world as the archetype of "primitive" or "Stone-Age" man. The reason why they should have been accorded this most dubious honor is not hard to discern: Aboriginal traditional culture differs dramatically from modern Western civilization. The earliest European adventurers to visit Australia concurred in their depiction of the Aborigines as the lowest of the low, "wild, cruel, black savages. . . poor and abject wretches," "the miserablest people in the world," ". . . setting aside their human shape, they differ but little from brutes."[1] In some early paintings they are portrayed as distinctly ape-like in posture and facial shape. They were seen to lack clothing, houses, villages, agriculture, domesticated animals, iron tools, and almost everything else a "civilized" people would need to survive. Worse, as people who were thought to represent the childhood of humanity itself, they were said to lack intellect, morality and — horror of horrors — religion. According to one writer in the 1880s, "It is a well-known fact that the Australian natives are almost wholly devoid of religious susceptibilities."[2] Western man, imbued with an unshakeable sense of racial and cultural superiority, was convinced that the Aborigines were living remnants of the earliest human societies on earth.

[1] Quoted by Moorehead (1967:109) from the records of Dutch explorers who visited the northwest coast in 1606, and of the English adventurer William Dampier who also visited the northwest in 1688.

[2] Attributed to a naturalist, Carl Lumholtz; quoted by Stanner (1965 a:208).

3

As more became known of them, and the many unique and fascinating features of Aboriginal culture were recognized by European scholars, the early views were modified, yet the simple-minded equation of technological development with intelligence and "civilization" has persisted in Western ethos. Aboriginal technology is certainly among the least elaborate of any people on earth, but Aboriginal forms of social organization and religious belief are exceedingly complex and very well integrated systems of thought and action; they stand as monuments to the triumph of culture over the limitations of a natural environment that is, in the desert at least, an extremely marginal one. The tragedy is that, even today, few white Australians are aware of or appreciate the genius of Aboriginal culture. Given white ignorance of Aboriginal culture, and given the immense technological gap that separates Aborigines from Western culture, no group could have been expected to have greater difficulty in adapting to the intrusion of the Western world.

Although the particular focus of this book is on culture contact between Aborigines and whites in a remote area of inland Australia, the situation described and analyzed here parallels that in many other parts of the world where nonliterate peoples are in contact with Western culture. In these frontier settings, acculturation has been predominantly a one-way process; nonliterate peoples have been led or forced into a subordinate status to colonizing whites and have suffered, in varying degrees, loss of traditional culture. Most of the world's small-scale societies are in transition, experiencing rapid and irreversible change as a result of the ubiquitous spread of Western culture. Whether this change is welcomed or resisted, non-Western people everywhere are struggling to retain their distinct identities amid the altered circumstances of their lives. Success in this struggle is never achieved easily, for while their survival depends greatly on their ability to maintain self-esteem and racial pride, they are soon made aware of their subordinate status as subject peoples, and this realization weakens their proud ethnocentrism. Many subject peoples, unable or unwilling to resist, have been pushed into a kind of spiritual and social limbo where they stagnate, bereft of much of their tradition and denied equal status within the colonizing society.

This widespread consequence of contact between Western and traditional peoples raises an important question: how can an ethnic minority in a dependent status maintain its cultural identity in the face of many forces in Western culture and in the contact situation which should cause it to disintegrate?

Because of their isolation in forbidding or marginal environments, some traditional peoples survived the initial traumas of contact and were not badly ravaged by disease and depopulation. Many such groups adapted to the new forces by developing various strategies aimed at resisting or at least cushioning pressures towards unwanted change. Once physical survival has ceased to be an issue and a method of living with the newcomers is established, the traditional people quickly accept their economic dependence on the whites but manipulate the situation in such a way that they preserve as many of their core values as possible. How effectively and for how long they can perform this balancing act depends on the particular circumstances of the contact situation.

Among the peoples who have been relatively successful in adjusting to Western cultural pressures are the Aborigines of Jigalong, a mission station in Western Australia that is the setting for this study (see Map 1). Formerly, these Aborigines exploited a desert environment by means of a semi-nomadic hunting and gathering adaptation that required them to move frequently and to cover large distances in search of food. Their sedentarization at Jigalong has led to important modifications in their culture, especially in their local organization and economic life. Yet despite their voluntary relocation in a different ecological niche and their increasing involvement in a money economy, these Aborigines have not suffered any serious breakdown in their kinship system or religious life.

The ability of Jigalong's Aborigines to remain predominantly tradition-oriented in the face of Westernization pressures is in sharp contrast to the rapid post-contact collapse of Aboriginal culture in most areas of Australia. This book attempts to explain this contrast by examining the nature and operation of adaptive strategies, which are the ways in which the Aborigines avoid costly compromises with whites, and maintain the belief that they alone control their destiny.

To understand the rationale behind the kinds of strategies that the Aborigines adopt and their method of implementation, it will be necessary to consider as well the nature of the white sub-cultures with which they interact most often, and the strategies

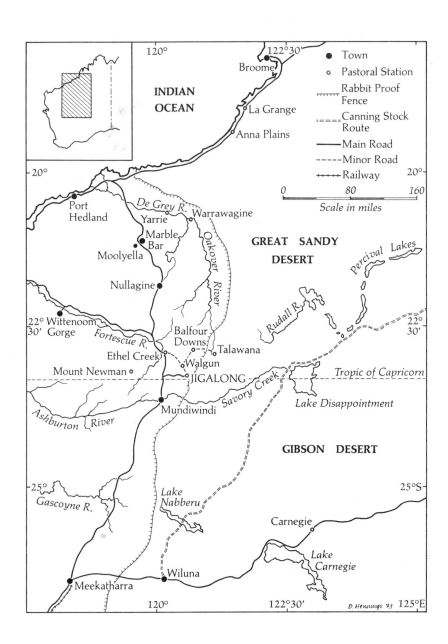

Map 1. North Central Area of Western Australia.

adopted by the whites in dealing with Aborigines. All too often in studies of contact between agents of Western culture and traditional peoples, the whites are treated as givens and are ignored in favor of the indigenous people who are undergoing change. An accurate assessment of the nature of conjunctive relations is possible only if the aspirations, motives, and behaviors of all participating groups are taken into account.

The kinds of role-stereotypes that develop as a result of prolonged culture contact have considerable influence upon the choice of adaptive strategies utilized by the groups involved. This is particularly true at Jigalong, where the two main groups concerned, Aborigines and missionaries, have clearly defined and mutually unfavorable stereotypes. It will be shown that the maintenance of such stereotypes has important survival value for both parties, bound together as they are in a relationship of necessary interdependence.

In the later discussion of adaptive strategies, several closely related factors will be considered. One is the effect of Aboriginal relocation and sedentarization on their social organization, specifically the emergence of what is for them a new kind of solidary grouping – the Jigalong mob. Another major factor is the pivotal role of the Aboriginal Law, which is exemplified most clearly in their kinship system and religious life.[3] The Law reinforces Aboriginal exclusiveness, racial pride, and sense of identity, and can thus be viewed as an effective defense against cultural breakdown. A third factor of major importance is the rejection of Christianity by Jigalong Aborigines.

Missions to the Aborigines have not been notably successful in converting them to the Christian faith, partly because of the strength of traditional religious beliefs but more importantly because of poor intercultural communication. Jigalong is a case in

---

[3] Following J. Wilson (1961), K. Wilson (1961, 1970) and later writers, I use the capitalized word Law to refer to the Aboriginal concept, which connotes a body of jural rules and moral evaluations of customary and socially sanctioned behavior patterns that are believed by the Aborigines to have originated in the creative period, the Dreamtime (see Chapter Four). The Aborigines use the English word at least as often as its dialect equivalent, *julubidi*. I use the term without a capital to refer to white Australian law. The Aborigines make a conceptual equation of the two systems and emphasize the use of rules and social control mechanisms in both.

which both parties deliberately perpetuate this poor communication as part of their respective adaptive strategies. As long as the messages remain confused and ambiguous, the Aborigines can exploit misunderstandings by extracting maximum concessions from the missionaries for a minimum physical output, while retaining the freedom to manage their own internal affairs. Faulty communication enables the missionaries to sustain untarnished their negative stereotype of the Aborigines and continue to rationalize their evangelical failures by laying the blame squarely on the Aborigines. These and other strategies are a principal concern of this study, because the Jigalong Aborigines' successful maintenance of cultural identity in the contact environment is best accounted for in terms of such strategies.

Because it would be difficult to understand much of what is happening at Jigalong without some background knowledge, the early chapters of this book provide a largely descriptive account of relevant historical and environmental factors as well as important aspects of traditional Aboriginal culture. Chapter Two outlines the natural and precontact cultural environment of the Western Desert and describes the circumstances and phases of cultural contact in the area. The chapter concludes with an account of the establishment and history of the Jigalong settlement up to the ethnographic present. This is a necessary prelude to Chapter Three, which is a synchronic description of the social, economic, and political organization of the community that identifies itself as the Jigalong mob. A major aim of the third chapter is to show that, despite the Aborigines' increasing involvement with and dependence upon whites in important economic aspects of their life, they remain tradition-oriented in key aspects of their social organization. Because there has been minimal interference in their internal affairs, the Aborigines maintain a feeling of political independence as well.

Since an adequate appreciation of Aboriginal culture is impossible without some knowledge of the complexities and genius of their religion and of its pervasive significance, Chapter Four describes in some detail the major features of the religious life of the Jigalong Aborigines. It is this aspect of their present existence that most clearly illustrates the Aborigines' commitment to traditional values. Religious beliefs and activities validate the truths embedded in the Law and constitute the most potent integrating force in the community that has evolved at the settlement. The Aborigines' sense of racial pride stems from their religion, so its continuance is vital to their cultural identity.

In providing the Aborigines with many new possible alternatives and additions to traditional culture, the contact situation confronts them with dilemmas of choice: whether to accept or reject the many Western cultural elements now available to them. Chapter Five is concerned with the kinds of foreign elements that the Aborigines of Jigalong have accepted and incorporated into their present culture. Predictably, items of material culture, particularly those of obvious and immediate utility, predominate and are found in both sacred and secular spheres of life; but many are modified by the Aborigines who use them. In addition, the behaviors and attitudes that are concomitant with the use of these things in Western culture are often absent at Jigalong.

Chapter Six focuses on Aboriginal-missionary conjunctive relations and attempts to account for the Jigalong Aborigines' rejection of Christianity. This involves a delineation of the main features of the missionary subculture, and of aspects of the contact situation that promote conflict-orientation between the two groups concerned. The various adaptive strategies of both groups are described to explain why the Aborigines and missionaries continue to coexist despite irreconcilable differences.

In the final chapter, the survival strategies which Jigalong's Aborigines use to cope with whites and with the wider society are summarized and evaluated. The role of the Law as a vital defense against cultural disintegration is discussed in view of important differences between Jigalong and other Aboriginal communities in the surrounding area. Finally, events at Jigalong are updated to include recent significant developments, and some predictions are made about what could happen to the Jigalong Aborigines in the foreseeable future.

Background to the Study

I spent a total of sixteen months at Jigalong between April 1963 and February 1970. During this time I made six trips to the settlement, staying from two weeks to six months each time. In addition, between 1963 and 1969, I made five brief trips into

the Western Desert area as an interpreter-advisor for the Native
Welfare Department, and one trip as a technical advisor for a
Commonwealth Film Unit crew.[4] Through these expeditions I
was able to gain some idea of what the traditional desert culture
had been like.

Earlier fieldwork among part-Aborigines in a small town in
the southwest region of Western Australia was both disquieting
and difficult for me, so I resolved to work among Aborigines who
were actively maintaining much of their traditional culture. I
chose Jigalong because little was known of the area anthropo-
logically, and its isolation suggested that acculturative pressures
there would be relatively light. My early fieldwork there (1963-
1966) was carried out while I was a graduate student at the
University of Western Australia, and it formed the basis for my
M.A. thesis (1966) which was a study of Aboriginal social structure and acculturation; part of this book stems from material first
presented in that thesis, and the ethnographic present tense refers
to the situation at Jigalong in the mid-1960s.

In the field, I gathered information using standard ethnographic methods: observation, interview, the collection of
genealogies, census information, crayon drawings, and life histo-
ries. Most interviews and conversations were in the local language
after the first field period. I used a tape recorder to collect songs,
language material, and activities such as public meetings and
fights, and took several thousand color and black-and-white photographs and four thousand feet of eight millimeter color movie film.

I arrived at Jigalong for the first field period at a time of
heightened tension between the Aborigines and missionaries there
and immediately became part of a situation fraught with problems
for the novice anthropologist. To gain rapport with the Aborigines I had to demonstrate that I was not a missionary, which I did
by avoiding mission religious services, by carrying tobacco (by
Aboriginal definition, "Christians" do not possess or smoke tobacco), and by using my normally rather blasphemous language.
My failure to attend church services upset the missionaries, who

---

[4] This trip resulted in the production of eleven films, "Desert People" and a
ten-part series entitled "People of the Australian Western Desert." These
films, which are available in the United States, depict aspects of the daily
life of two Aboriginal families in their desert environment.

were not enthusiastic about my presence anyway because my keen interest in traditional cultural elements might encourage the Aborigines to believe that some of their traditions were worth retaining. Since I had to remain at least partially acceptable to the missionaries, on whom I was dependent for certain things, I maintained polite relationships with them. But my sympathies lay very strongly with the Aborigines, and my unhappiness about many of the missionaries' attitudes and behavior towards them, as well as my suspected status as a nonbeliever, led me to avoid prolonged contact with the missionaries. At times when missionaries did seek advice on improving relations with the Aborigines, I readily gave it but soon realized that my advice was paid lip-service, then ignored at the practical level.

I was caught in the classic middleman position, as both parties attempted to justify their positions and sought my agreement with their viewpoints. Both used me at times to convey messages and to sound out the opposition's possible reactions to new developments. This made for a strenuous six months, complicated by my ignorance of the nature of culture shock. Visitors to the mission were few, so I looked forward eagerly to the arrival of mail and to the periodic visits of the Flying Doctor Service airplane. Several times I was so desperate for "one of my own kind" to talk to that I practically chased the plane down the strip, so that I could bend the ear of a sympathetic outsider.

In view of my description later in this book of the missionary subculture at Jigalong, I should say that my general dislike of the missionaries as a group did not extend to all. I became quite friendly with one couple, with whom I stayed during subsequent field trips, and we are still close friends. I do not think that Jigalong is typical of Australian missions, and judging by my later experiences while doing research in Melanesia, I do not consider the Jigalong missionaries to be at all typical of Australian missionaries in general.

CHAPTER TWO

Environmental and Historical Setting

Covering an area of at least 500,000 square miles, the Western Desert (Map 2) occupies a vast region in the interior of Australia. This general area has long been, by Western standards at least, a most unattractive and inhospitable environment. It was recently described as "probably the most undependable and impoverished habitat anywhere in the world where people have succeeded in living entirely off the land" (Gould 1971:145).

A traveler entering the desert for the first time cannot help being overawed by its immensity and its inhospitable vibrations, particularly in summer. One wonders how anybody could survive here, let alone maintain a complex and lively culture. Yet, in an environment that appears to have been as arid and unrelenting 10,000 years ago as it is now, several thousand Aborigines sustained a hunting and gathering adaptation that allowed them much leisure time for social and ceremonial activities.[1]

Although several contiguous named deserts (Map 2) comprise the Western Desert, all share similar physiographic features. The most common landforms are seemingly-endless, parallel sandridges, forty to eighty feet high and running roughly east-west. Most are covered with small shrubs and spikey spinifex grass that

---

[1] The precontact population of the Western Desert is virtually impossible to assess, and the present population is not accurately known owing to a lack of reliable census material and the fact that a few Aborigines are still moving about frequently. R. and C. Berndt suggest an approximate figure of 2,000 in the Western Australian section (1970:64). If the rest of the Western Desert is included, the population would probably exceed 4,000.

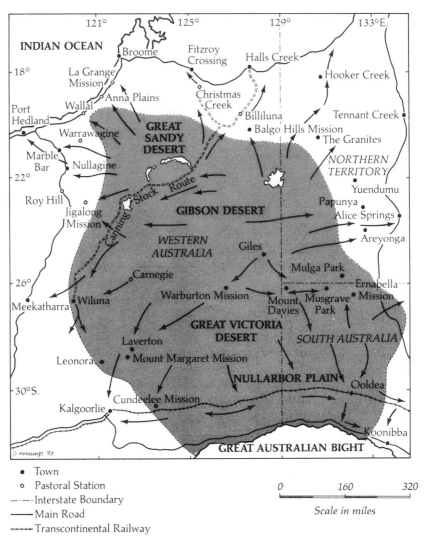

- • Town
- ○ Pastoral Station
- —·—· Interstate Boundary
- ——— Main Road
- ++++ Transcontinental Railway

0   160   320

Scale in miles

NOTE: The dotted lines indicate the approximate boundaries of the Western Desert cultural bloc. The arrows indicate the directions of Aboriginal migration in the Western Desert area.

Map 2. **The Western Desert Area of Australia.**

is uncomfortable for the careless walker. Between the ridges is flat sandplain dotted with spinifex, small bushes, a few ghostgum trees, and occasional desert oaks (casuarina) whose height, often in excess of thirty feet, is amazing in view of the paucity of rainfall.

The monotony of the sandridges is broken in places by outcrops of low rugged sandstone and quartzite hills, covered with irregularly-sized boulders and spinifex. Such hills are often surrounded by stands of dense mulga (acacia) scrub or by gibber plains, whose surface consists of very small rounded stones interspersed with clumps of spinifex. Radiating from hilly areas are creekbeds in which water flows for brief periods after rain; many are lined with large river-gum trees, acacia shrubs, and various grasses. In some areas these creekbeds lead to large salt flats, which become lakes after heavy rain but are generally useless as sources of potable water.

Daily and seasonal temperatures vary considerably in the desert. Shade temperatures in summer range from 80°F. to 125°F. but are made bearable much of the time by the extreme dryness of the air. Winter temperatures vary from below 30°F. to about 80°F. with days that are usually sunny and warm once the early morning chill dissipates. The average annual rainfall is between five and ten inches, but falls are so erratic that such figures are almost meaningless. A given area's total rainfall for several years may be one or two inches, then in one cyclonic storm over ten inches may fall in a matter of hours. Most of the rain that falls occurs in summer; it is associated with violent thunderstorm activity, high winds, threatening skies, raging duststorms, but very little effective precipitation since most evaporates before reaching the ground. Except for brief periods immediately following heavy rain, when surface water may be abundant, Aborigines must rely heavily on sheltered rockholes, creekbed soaks, and native wells for drinking water.

For such a marginal environment, the desert is surprisingly rich in bird, insect, and animal life. For example, in the Jigalong area on the western fringe of the desert proper, some forty-five species of birds are found (Lindgren 1961:174). Western Desert Aborigines, whose principal source of protein is small game (especially lizards and introduced animals such as rabbits, feral cats, foxes, and field mice), hunt or collect at least forty-seven species of animals, including certain edible grubs and insects (Gould 1971: 146). Vegetable foods, which were probably more important to the traditional subsistence economy than meat, come from about fifty edible plant species which provide food in the form of tree and grass seeds, berries, fruits, and tubers.

Correlated with the physiographic and climatic commonalities of the Western Desert are its uniformities as a cultural bloc (cf. Berndt 1963:393-394). Its Aboriginal inhabitants speak a common language with dialectical variations and share a similar basic social organization, relationship to the natural environment, religion, mythology, and artistic expression.[2] The relatively homogeneous nature of Western Desert culture is evident from the available literature, and recent ethnoarchaeological findings suggest that, technologically at least, cultural continuities have existed in this area from several thousand years ago to the present (Gould 1971:174).

Any traveler who is familiar with Western Desert culture and who speaks one of its dialects will notice obvious similarities among widely separated groups of Aborigines within the cultural bloc. I traveled extensively in the area and could make myself understood everywhere using the dialect I had learned. I encountered many identical kinship terms in use, and although they did not always connote the same classes of relatives in different areas, they formed part of the same type of social organization. Also, many of the rituals and associated ancestral beings were substantially the same in areas hundreds of miles apart. The regular contact between contiguous Aboriginal groups in the Western Desert that has always been a feature of the area ensures a steady flow of information and objects. This cultural transmission reinforces the Aborigines' awareness of their common interests and helps give the Western Desert its markedly homogeneous countenance.

---

[2] For further information on Western Desert culture, see: C. Berndt 1965: 238-282; R. and C. Berndt 1945, 1964, 1970:53-79; R. Berndt 1959:81-107, 1963:393-394, 1970: 216-247; Douglas 1958; Gould 1968:101-122, 1969a, 1969b:253-274, 1970a, 1970b:56-67, 1971:143-177, 1972:17-22; Long 1964a:72-82, 1964b:24-35; 1971:262-270; Meggitt 1962, 1966; Munn 1965, 1970:141-163, 1973; Strehlow 1965:121-145; Yengoyan 1970:70-91.

The Precontact Culture

In the following paragraphs I use the few reports of early observers — sketchy as they are — together with what is known of traditional elements in the existing culture, to recreate the essential features of precontact Western Desert culture.

The desert Aborigines possessed a Stone-Age technology and sustained themselves by hunting and gathering activities in an area that is decidedly marginal for man, even when compared to the homelands of most other hunter-gatherer societies. They are characterized as being seminomadic rather than nomadic for good reason: although often forced to cover large areas because of scattered food and water resources, the Aborigines had a strong emotional and religious attachment to a specific stretch of territory, and within it, to their place of birth and certain sacred sites.

A useful distinction can be made between this home area or "estate," which is the traditional heartland of a local group, and its "range," the area usually exploited by group members in the course of their hunting and gathering activities (Stanner 1965:2). Initiated male agnates (paternal kin) in each local group shared special responsibilities towards the maintenance of certain sacred sites in its estate. People belonging to this exogamous, patrilineal, landholding group traveled as members of hordes. Beyond its core of patrilineally related kinsmen and their families, the horde group was changeable in composition; it varied frequently in size and in some of its membership.[3] For much of the year the horde was necessarily small in order to sustain itself in areas of limited food resources. It consisted typically of from one to three patrilineally linked families, who might be joined at times by affines (relatives by marriage) or young initiates and their older escorts.

The linguistic unit was a larger and more readily defined social unit, named for the dialect spoken by its members and com-

---

[3] In making this distinction between the horde and the local patrilineal group I follow R. Berndt (1957:346-351; 1959:95-104), but I should point out that there has been considerable debate over the true nature of the horde in Aboriginal Australia. Interested readers should see: Radcliffe-Brown 1930-1931; Hiatt 1962:267-286, 1966:81-92; Meggitt 1962; and Stanner 1965b:1-26.

posed of several contiguous local groups interrelated by marriage. Normally, such a unit occupied a specific area, with known but not precisely defined borders. Members of the linguistic unit generally came together once or twice a year, often in combination with members of neighboring units. At these meetings, the Aborigines held initiation and other rituals, settled grievances, gave women in marriage, planned future meetings, exchanged items of trade and religious material, and passed on information. After these gatherings, which lasted from several days to weeks, the various groups would separate and head for their home areas.[4]

This pattern of dispersal-aggregation-dispersal, so typical of Aboriginal culture, was a necessary human response to the unpredictable and fluctuating availability of plant and water resources. These factors determined whether or not such meetings could take place, where, and for how long.[5]

The Aborigines were not warlike. The periodic uncertainty of water and food supplies made it necessary to maintain good relations with their neighbors, who might provide vital access to food resources. Besides, contiguous peoples were invariably kinsmen through the operation of classificatory kinship (see Chapter Three), and they shared many common cultural bonds in addition to their mutually intelligible dialects. They were also links in a chain of cultural transmission which was contingent upon the Aborigines' acknowledgement of shared basic values and similar conceptions of their cosmic order.

During the course of its daily subsistence activities, the family maintained a fairly loose sexual division of labor: the husband and older sons hunted large game while the wives and children gathered vegetable foods and small game which formed the bulk

---

[4] I have deliberately avoided using the term "tribe" to describe any Western Desert grouping. R. Berndt has shown that the term is not applicable to any social unit found in the region (1959:104). The large group that periodically gathers for "big meetings" is termed by Berndt the "religious unit," the widest functionally significant social grouping found in the Western Desert area.

[5] Most aggregations probably occurred after heavy rains had brought about an abundance of water and food supplies in the chosen area. However, Long suggests that larger groups may have also come together in the hot dry summer months at more reliable wells where shade and good water were available (1971:265)

of the family's diet. Provision of big game, such as kangaroos and emus, depended on the luck of the hunt. Contrary to earlier assertions about hunting and gathering peoples, we now know that the task of obtaining daily food rarely occupied more than a few hours of the Aborigines' time.[6] In summer at least, the intense heat discouraged Aborigines from moving about during most of the day. Their leisure hours were many, whatever the season, and the opportunities to be sociable were endless. Horde members were constantly on the lookout for telltale smoke, which indicated the presence of other small groups. The resultant meeting generated excitement as people exchanged gossip, recounted their recent exploits, and perhaps held informal singing and dancing sessions.

Aboriginal survival in an adverse physical environment depended upon an intimate knowledge of available resources and an ability to time their moves to coincide with the presence of sufficient water and food. Because of uncertain rainfall distribution, the pattern of movement within any particular year was never duplicated. To the outsider, this existence appears very precarious, but the Aborigines' religious world view provided a sense of well-being and security. They felt certain that rain would fall, plants would grow, and animals would breed each year, if they performed certain rituals aimed at securing the continued cooperation of the natural world through the mediating activities of spiritual beings. The Aborigines saw man and nature as a continuum, mutually dependent and in agreement. All were linked with creative spiritual beings in a unified cosmic order; natural and supernatural realms were indistinguishable.

An observer who travels with Aborigines through their home territory is soon aware that perceptions of the desert differ. The Aborigine sees his home as a marvelous, supportive place, full of waterholes and with some kind of food always available. It is composed of physiographic features that abound in religious significance because he knows how they came into existence during the great formative period, the Dreamtime (see Chapter Four). Because all these landforms were created by ancestral beings with whom he strongly identifies as relatives and supporters, the Aborigine feels secure in his homeland.

---

[6] See, for example, the discussions in *Man the Hunter* (1968), and Sahlins 1972:14-32).

Plate 1. Minma, a Western Desert Aborigine, heaps wood for a fire while sons Nu:n and Djambidjin play with the dead kangaroo which their father is preparing to cook.

Only in recent years has the Western Desert attracted the attention of scholars interested in unlocking secrets of its cultural past. Although no comprehensive archaeological research has been done in the Western Desert, excavations at a site in the central area indicate that it has been continuously inhabited for the past 10,000 years and suggest that the Aborigines have maintained a stable hunting and gathering adaptation for at least as long (Gould 1971:174). Available genetic evidence implies that the Aborigines of the Western Desert have been in isolation for a long

Plate 2. A Western Desert family sets out for a day of hunting and gathering in spinifex grass and mulga scrub country. Minma carries his spears, thrower, and a firestick.

Plate 3. Co-wives Mangadji and Janindu help balance their wooden dishes with pads made of emu feathers. Janindu (right) carries a grinding stone in her dish and has a digging stick in her hand.

period; apparently there was no gene flow from the coast to the interior (Kirk 1971:335). Although some trading took place with their neighbors along the desert edges, the Aborigines of the Western Desert cultural bloc appear to have experienced a long period of cultural stability with minimal outside interference. With the coming of whites, however, their desert culture began to undergo profound transformation.

History of Culture Contact

Apart from contacts between some Aboriginal groups on the north coast and visiting Macassan and Papuan traders (none of whom are known to have settled there), Aboriginal Australia remained isolated for many thousands of years. After their initial settlement on the east coast in 1788, British colonists rapidly occupied the more fertile areas of the continent in the east and south, then later moved further inland. Traditional Aboriginal culture was ill-equipped to deal with the unexpected, especially of this magnitude. Suddenly confronted with technologically superior and aggressive intruders, the Aborigines were forced continually to give ground. Their culture rapidly collapsed under the combined effects of physical attacks, disease, deprivation, and a resulting loss of the will to live.

Most whites were completely ignorant of the nature of Aboriginal culture, and, imbued as they were with the belief that the Aborigines were little better than animals, they were generally uncompromising and unsympathetic. In the fertile areas of eastern, southern and southwestern Australia, Aboriginal culture reacted to the trauma of contact by falling apart. The Aborigines' semi-nomadic activities were thwarted, and the few pitiful survivors adapted to a life of pauperism in the fringes of white society.[7]

Culture contact in the Western Desert, however, was quite different from that in the more fertile and climatically equable regions of Australia. For a long time after the latter areas had been settled and their Aboriginal inhabitants decimated, the West-

---

[7] The best integrated and most detailed account of the destruction of Aboriginal society is given in an excellent book by Rowley (1970). For a brief, readable account see Moorehead (1967).

ern Desert remained untouched except for brief expeditions made by explorers and prospectors in the late 1800s. The absence of lasting surface waters, the unreliable rainfall, intensely hot summers, difficulties of communication, and high cost of transport discouraged whites from venturing there. Thus, because of the isolation and the uninviting nature of their homeland, desert Aborigines were never displaced or depopulated as a direct result of alien intrusion. The contact situation was atypical in that, initially at least, the Aborigines had the choice of either seeking or avoiding contact with whites. In most cases they had to move towards perpiheral areas if they wished to interact with the newcomers.

The desert Aborigines were also fortunate in having time to accustom themselves to the idea of the presence of whites and to learn about them before actually making contact. They could do this because Aborigines in contact areas traded Western goods into the desert and passed on information about the newcomers. It appears that they were motivated more by sheer curiosity than anything else in deciding to go and meet the whites (cf. Meggitt 1962:336). The frontier in this part of Australia was largely a peaceful one; the few whites were outnumbered by Aborigines and dependent on them for labor.

In the early years of this century, small outposts — pastoral stations, mining settlements, railheads, and missions — were founded along the desert periphery. Subsequently, these settlements attracted groups of Aboriginal immigrants from the desert. This outward movement continued until the present time when only a handful of Aborigines remain in the interior away from contact with whites. Map 2 illustrates the migration routes of Western Desert Aborigines.

The pattern of Aboriginal-white contact seems to have been similar throughout the desert area. Aborigines moving into settlements for the first time usually had no intention of remaining there permanently, and certainly had no conception of the long-term consequences of their action (cf. R. and C. Berndt 1964: 439). In the early stages, only those local Aborigines who had lost control of their home territory congregated around the settlements as indigents or casual laborers. Aborigines from further afield began to visit, but they initially stayed only long enough to see their relatives and obtain food until rains brought about fresh plant growth in their home areas. Many seemed content to continue this sporadic pattern of contact indefinitely; it enabled them to maintain their independence yet allowed them to obtain useful material goods which they had come to value.

In poor seasons, visiting groups prolonged their stay in the settlements. As they became more accustomed to the contact milieu, they were less inclined to return to the more arduous desert life, until finally they found themselves unwilling to make the break and return to their home territories. As the desert population dwindled, the number of Aborigines remaining eventually became too small for the proper enactment of rituals — especially initiations — and for the continuance of customary marriage arrangements. For many Aborigines, though, it was perhaps the combination of severe droughts and an increasing desire for tea, sugar, and other Western goods that led them eventually to become permanent fringe dwellers.

At the settlements, the immigrants were usually assured of a supply of foreign foods and goods in exchange for doing odd jobs such as woodchopping and laundry work. Many Aboriginal men were trained as ranch-hands and became skilled workers, while some women became cooks and domestics. On many frontier properties, white bachelors relied on Aboriginal women as sexual partners, and the stable relationships so formed were instrumental in maintaining peaceful interracial relationships in remote areas. Many settlements, especially missions, attracted sizeable Aboriginal populations largely because they acted as government food distribution centers authorized to allocate regular supplies of food and clothing to indigent Aborigines. At missions attempts were also made to educate the children and indoctrinate the Aborigines with some form of Christianity.

Today, almost all Western Desert Aborigines are congregated in fringe settlements, or even further afield in small towns. Although physically separated from their desert homelands, most maintain close spiritual ties with their birthplace and earlier life. Every settlement contains Aborigines from several different linguistic groups and areas of origin, yet its Aborigines share the same kinship system, religious life, and general cultural background. These commonalities are major integrative forces and promote feelings of settlement unity. Although a small proportion of Aborigines at every settlement are transients who move freely among neighboring communities, most identify strongly with one particular settlement.

All fringe settlements share certain common features, despite considerable geographical separation, and the social situation that has evolved is remarkably similar throughout the area. Many settlements lie within designated Native Reserves, to which entry is illegal for all but authorized aliens, although Aborigines can go and come as they please.[8] Basic economic changes have occurred everywhere: while Aborigines continue to supplement Western food with hunting and gathering activities, they are dependent on the whites for continued subsistence. Few settlement Aborigines still retain the ability or inclination to return to their former desert existence for more than very brief periods. Educational facilities have brought literacy to the younger people, an increased awareness of the wider world, and a small measure of vocational training, but nowhere in the desert periphery are there sufficient employment opportunities for all the Aborigines who need work. Improved medical care has lowered both infant and adult mortality rates, and the entire area is experiencing a minor population explosion.[9]

Improved roads and the acquisition of motor vehicles by Western Desert Aborigines have made it easier to maintain intercommunity cultural transmission, with the consequence that Aborigines from neighboring settlements hundreds of miles apart are in frequent contact. In all settlements, there has been ready acceptance of many Western material goods, but there has also been a determined retention of native languages and, in varying degrees, of traditional nonmaterial cultural forms. In some areas, where the Aborigines have ready access to liquor, considerable social problems have arisen and traditional cultural elements are undergoing accelerated breakdown.

---

[8] In Australia not even the Native Reserves are owned by the Aborigines; they are all Crown land. The recently elected Labor government, however, has promised to give urgent consideration to the problem of Aboriginal land rights.

[9] This is only part of an Australia-wide trend in rapid Aboriginal population increase; cf. Jones (1970).

Jigalong

Jigalong is a relatively isolated mission on the western edge of the Gibson Desert in the north central area of the state of Western Australia (see Map 1). The main settlement lies on flat ground near the confluence of two sizeable creekbeds; to the west are low undulating hills and to the east are broken ridges. The original vegetation consisted of thickets of mulga trees interspersed with shrubs and grassland, but considerable denudation has occurred in the vicinity of the settlement. Trees and grasses have been depleted by drought, overgrazing, and the Aborigines' use of wood for fires and weapon making. The general absence of vegetation cover allows winds to carry away the topsoil, and minor dust storms make the main Aboriginal camp extremely unpleasant at times. The barren landscape is transformed only after heavy rains which cause a great variety of wildflowers, grasses and small shrubs to appear. This revitalized vegetation is a source of wild foods for those Aborigines interested in gathering them. Most years, game animals are fairly abundant in the surrounding countryside; of these, kangaroos, emus, scrub turkeys, galahs (a kind of parrot), and lizards are most commonly hunted by Aborigines who want to supplement their normal diet of Western foods.

Although the flora around Jigalong is semi-desert in type, the area's temperature and rainfall are characteristic of the desert. Rainfall, averaging about six inches annually, is extremely erratic but shows regular cyclic patterns of a good year followed by several dry ones (Lindgren 1961:169-170). There is a tendency for a maximum rainfall in summer, but in most years there is some winter rain. The settlement's water supply comes by pipeline from windmills on bores about a mile away, but because these tap relatively small reservoirs, water shortages sometimes occur until rain falls and the Aborigines can draw water from creekbed soaks.

The settlement itself lies within a Native Reserve of 500,000 acres, but total mission holdings amount to about 1,250,000 acres. Map 3 shows a plan of the settlement, which consists in its built-up section of two clusters of buildings along a central "street," with a government school near the central area. The bed of Jigalong Creek separates the settlement buildings from the Aboriginal Camp (hereafter referred to as "the Camp" to distinguish it from individual camps or campsites).

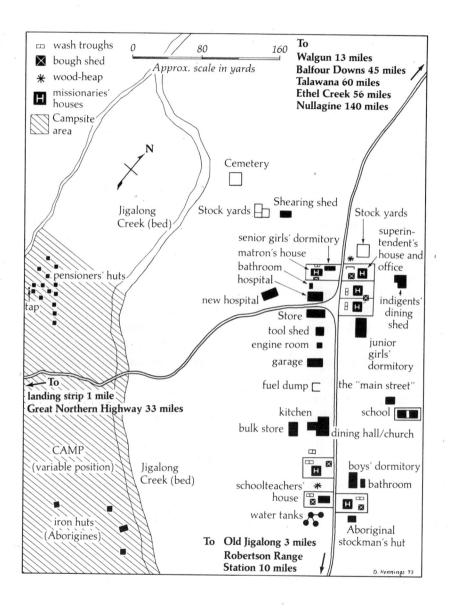

Map 3. Plan of Jigalong Mission.

All school-age Aboriginal children are housed in the three dormitories and take their meals in the dining room. They have only limited daily access to the Camp, during which time they can visit with their families. The location of the boys' and girls' dormitories at opposite ends of the mission is deliberate and is aimed at minimizing clandestine sexual liaisons. At the indigents' dining shed, meals are served to pensioners and Aboriginal mission workers. An Aboriginal female kitchen staff cooks midday meals for the workers and all meals for the schoolchildren. The store, patronized by Aborigines, missionaries, and a few neighboring station people, is owned and operated by the mission as a commercial enterprise. The bough sheds are grass-walled, water-cooled shelters (common in the North West area) which afford whites relief from the intense summer heat.

The settlement is linked to the outside world only by poor-quality gravel roads that are impassible after heavy rains and by daily radio contact, so communications are tenuous. The mission truck makes regular trips to collect supplies from the railhead at Meekatharra, 300 miles south, and a truck delivers mail every two weeks. Because it is somewhat off the beaten track, the mission has negligible through-traffic and receives few visitors apart from Aborigines and government officials. The local airfield is used by the Royal Flying Doctor Service aircraft which visit the settlement monthly and at other times to evacuate seriously ill people to a hospital on the coast.

The Pre-Mission Period. Although Jigalong was not founded until 1907, the desert area to the east was traversed by several explorers prior to the end of the nineteenth century. Little is known of encounters between these travelers and Aborigines; no bloody interracial confrontations are recorded for this area before the early 1900s. One explorers, Wells, noted that Aborigines had stripped a camp belonging to two whites who had died of thirst, taking everything they perceived as useful. He later saw trouser fabric being used as a pubic cover and a sharpened saddle bow made into an axe (Wells 1902).

In 1906-1907 a party of whites laid out a thousand-mile chain of wells, the Canning Stock Route, which linked pastoral areas in the north to the railhead at Wiluna, via the Western Desert (see Map 2). In the process, two kinds of events aroused the enmity of the desert Aborigines: members of the construction party committed several acts of cruelty to Aborigines they caught, and in excavating native wells they unwittingly desecrated sacred sites. One white was fatally speared, apparently because he took possession of a bundle of sacred objects belonging to local Aborigines. The first two whites to use the stock route in later years were speared to death, and subsequent police punitive expeditions for a time intensified the Aborigines' distrust of intruding whites.

Although the stock route was barely used by whites, it had important effects on the movements of Aborigines through whose territories it passed. Because of the certainty of obtaining water and game along the route, the Aborigines used it to travel much further afield than they had traveled traditionally, and such trips inevitably took them closer to white settlements.

For Jigalong people, the stock route has become a convenient reference point for locating the approximate position of birthplaces and important sites, and many of the younger people were born near its wells. Most members of the Mandjildjara speakers, the linguistic group now numerically dominant at the mission, traveled south along the route which straddles their original territory, and then either headed westwards to Jigalong or continued south to Wiluna.[10] Other Mandjildjara went northwards along the route, and as a result of such diverse movements, members of this linguistic group are now scattered over a much larger area than they were traditionally.[11]

The construction of the No. 1 Rabbit Proof Fence (a futile attempt to prevent rabbits from invading certain areas of the continent) gave rise to Jigalong. Completed in 1907, the fence was maintained by regular patrols which operated from small depots

---

[10] To transcribe Aboriginal words used in this book, I follow the practice adopted in earlier publications (e.g. Tonkinson 1970). There are seventeen consonant phonemes: b, dj, ḍ, d, g, m, nj, ṇ, n, ŋ, lj, ḷ, l, ṛ, r, w, j (pronounced y); the sublineal dots indicate retroflexed sounds (as in the English r sound). There are three short vowels: a, i, u; and three lengthened vowels: a:, i:, u:. For a full description of the phonemic system, see Douglas (1958).

[11] Map 4 shows the Jigalong Aborigines' perception of the relative locations of all linguistic groups known to them.

established along it. Jigalong, one such depot, was also a camel-breeding center until the 1930s when motor vehicles were introduced for patrol work.[12]   Located in an area of favorable water and game supplies, the Jigalong depot began to attract local Aboriginal groups, most of whose older members soon settled there. Because of this, the depot superintendent was made a Protector of Natives, authorized to issue rations to the nearby Aborigines. The staff, which consisted of two white men, employed as many Aborigines as possible in return for the ration handouts, and relations between the two groups were generally amicable. In the 1930s the depot began to attract desert people, who in time made up the bulk of the settlement population as the original local Aborigines drifted to pastoral stations further west.

Cattle and sheep stations were first established during the latter part of the last century in more favorable areas west of Jigalong. By the early 1900s pastoralists were taking up more marginal land further east, until their spread was halted by the western fringes of the desert proper. The contact situation at these outlying stations was similar in many respects to that at Jigalong. Most of the whites were bachelors who relied on the Aboriginal labor they had trained and on Aboriginal women for sexual gratification. Small groups of Aborigines congregated at each station and in time identified themselves with that place, unless maltreatment caused them to flee. The frontier was rough, yet the symbiotic nature of the relationship between station whites and "their" Aborigines was such that conflicts were not common. The Aborigines rapidly developed tastes for certain Western foods, especially tea, sugar, and flour, which they were increasingly reluctant to forsake by returning permanently to the desert. Even today, the longest desert trips made by settlement Aborigines on foot usually last about three weeks at most until their tea and sugar supplies are exhausted.

Most station whites knew or understood little about non-material aspects of traditional Aboriginal culture. Except for certain "exotic" customs, such as subincision, penis-holding rites, and

---

[12] Camels were introduced to Australia during the last century for transportation work in the interior. Some wild camels still roam in the desert area.

alleged cannibalism, the whites evinced little interest.[13] Nor did these whites try to interfere with or alter elements of Aboriginal culture as long as their employees worked as directed and made no trouble. The Aborigines were thus free to do what they liked in their leisure time; their kinship system functioned much as before, and they occupied much time with discussions and activities pertaining to the religious life. Many Aborigines learned to play cards while on stations, but it did not become a major leisure-time activity for many years.

Until about the mid-1950s, Aboriginal workers at most stations were not paid wages, but instead worked for food, clothing, tobacco, and certain desired material goods. They lived in bush camps, hunted in their spare time, and interacted minimally with their employers outside working hours. The only exceptions to this were women who were housegirls and sexual partners of white men. Such women usually enjoyed a higher status and had free access to the homestead, to which entry was denied other women and all males.

---

[13] Cannibalism was never an important feature of Aboriginal culture, but the Australian public believed it was, largely because of sensationalist exaggerations by certain writers, particularly Bates (1938). Subincision, which is practiced by many desert peoples in Aboriginal Australia, involves the cutting of the ventral surface of the penis, which is slit open from its orifice to one or two inches along the shaft, to expose the urethra. Medically it is termed "artificial hypospadias"; early white observers called it "the terrible rite" and it is known by local whites as "whistlecock." Contrary to popular belief, it is not a contraceptive measure but is a religious act done in emulation of ancestral creative beings who are said to have done the same thing to their penises during the Dreamtime. In the Jigalong area it is done in emulation of the emu (this large flightless bird has a distinct penile groove) and the songs associated specifically with the rite concern Galaja, the emu ancestors. For an excellent account of the meaning of subincision to Aborigines and for critiques of earlier theories, see Cawte et al. (1966:245-253). The operation itself is less important than subsequent blood letting from the urethra and subincision's significance as *the* sign of manhood. While space does not allow a description of the significance of the penis-holding rite in dispute settlements, the rite itself involves men pushing their partially erect penises down onto the upturned palms of other men, "proving" the existence of their subincision and therefore of their right to be present among initiated men. (For a fuller description of the rite, see R. and C. Berndt 1945:328-334.)

Many Jigalong adults first came into contact with whites at Talawana and Balfour Downs (see Map 1). These outlying stations are close to a major waterhole route from the desert to Jigalong and have served as staging places for Aborigines moving westward. These stations could support only small groups of Aborigines, so most of the immigrants soon moved on to Jigalong, where food rations were available.

Jigalong had certain advantages over other settlements (its then reliable water supply, its status as a ration depot and its nucleus of Aboriginal elders), which made it the most popular venue for annual festivities. These so-called "big meetings," modeled on similar traditional aggregations, attracted large numbers of Aborigines from different areas. Since these meetings centered on the performance of rituals, elders (the ritual leaders and custodians of sacred paraphernalia) had to be present. Most of the important sacred objects had been brought from their hiding places in the desert homeland and were now stored near the settlement. Evidence of the emergence of Jigalong as the center for traditional ritual activities in the area was the relocation, over the years, of various small stores of sacred objects from the vicinity of outlying stations into the secret storehouses at Jigalong.

The Mission Period. When maintenance of the Rabbit Proof Fence ceased in 1945 and the Jigalong depot was closed down, the state government offered it as a mission site to the Apostolic Church of Australia, a small Protestant fundamentalist sect which had been negotiating since 1941 to establish a mission in this area. The offer was accepted in December 1945, and an initial reserve of 16,000 acres was claimed, to be augmented later through the acquisition of some vacant neighboring station holdings. In 1948 the Native Welfare Department acquired the old depot buildings and gave them to the mission.

A 1947 Native Welfare report listed the Aboriginal population of the mission as 104, and said that the Aborigines lived with "all tribal customs upheld." In addition to the eight missionaries, two Aborigines were employed as laborers. Once a week, the rest of the adult Aborigines received a government ration issue, which they supplemented as before by hunting and gathering activities. The missionaries, following the example of the depot managers, employed as many Aborigines as possible so that they would earn their rations. Very few of the Aborigines living at the mission in

1947 ever returned to the desert. Instead, they were joined at Jigalong by their relatives who immigrated in later years.

The missionaries dispensed medical care and rations, but their main aim was to save the souls of the Aborigines, whom they considered "children of the devil" and "lost in darkness." Their strategy was to concentrate on the children, whose supposedly malleable and impressionable minds made them the most suitable subjects for later conversion. The missionaries placed all school-age children in dormitories. This policy had a twofold purpose; it provided the missionaries with a captive audience, and it partially separated the children from their parents and what the missionaries considered to be the pernicious influences of Camp life. In addition to these educative and evangelistic activities, the missionaries were charged with the operation of Jigalong as a pastoral concern.

The Aboriginal adults apparently accepted the presence of the newcomers and the removal of their children from the Camp. At that time they were unaware of the motives and methods of the missionaries. Church services were held regularly for the Aboriginal adults, who sometimes attended in the early years. Informants recalling the period told me, "We went to see what they did, to find out about these white people, but we couldn't 'hear' (understand) their talk — it was all in their language!"

From the start much of the ambition of the church leaders who administered the mission from Melbourne (in southeast Australia) was thwarted by problems that continued to plague the mission in later years: staff shortages, a high staff turnover rate, and inadequately trained personnel who were unprepared for life and work in this rigorous environment. But the missionaries battled on and administered a settlement population that kept increasing. By the mid-1950s there were about 160 Aborigines at the mission, and much of this increase was accounted for by the arrival of more desert groups, mostly Mandjildjara-speaking people.

As a result of the growing demand for seasonal labor on neighboring stations, the mission came to function as a labor pool for a wide area. Evidence of friction between the missionaries and some station whites soon appeared. Graziers began to complain that the mission was employing station-trained Aborigines towards the end of the midsummer slack season (November to February, the time of the annual "big meetings" at Jigalong), and was discouraging them from returning to their stations. In denying these allegations, the missionaries claimed that there was anti-mission prejudice among neighboring whites, especially the bachelors who did not want their housegirls employed elsewhere.

Tension between the missionaries and their white neighbors was inevitable. The two groups represented opposing lifestyles in many important respects. For religious reasons, the missionaries were solidly against smoking, swearing, the consumption of alcohol, illicit cohabitation, and any kind of extramarital sexual activity, blasphemy, ungodliness, such as the breaking of the Sabbath, failure to pray daily and worship in church regularly. Most local whites were firmly opposed to such proscriptions and considered many of these behaviors essential for their continued survival and sanity in an isolated environment.

Of considerable importance to the later discussion of adaptive strategies (see Chapter Six) is the fact that most of the Aborigines gathered at Jigalong had become accustomed to the station-white ethic. Their stereotype of the "whitefella" was defined largely in terms of their experience with station whites. It is thus not difficult to imagine the bewilderment of the Aborigines when a new group of aliens, the missionaries, appeared and sought to persuade them that everything associated with the stations was extremely sinful. This paradox was later compounded by the Aborigines' observation of frequent discrepancies between what the missionaries preached and what they practiced. The Aborigines came to perceive the missionaries as a special category of humans, different from all other whites; the "Christian-whitefella" dichotomy that resulted is discussed in Chapter Six.

Most graziers saw the presence of the mission as a potential threat, because the missionaries were opposed to their sexual relationships with Aboriginal women and their allegedly heathenish behavior. The husbands of the women concerned were apparently much less perturbed by these activities, since in most cases they gained material advantages from the arrangement. They were not morally shocked, because some kinds of extramarital sexual relationships were permissible in the traditional culture. Whatever the reasons, antagonism between the missionaries and their station neighbors has, with one or two exceptions, continued to affect their interaction, mainly by diminishing it.

In the early 1950s, an Aboriginal cooperative movement called Pindan was formed in the Port Hedland area (see Map 1). Pindan rapidly spread its influence in surrounding pastoral areas as its members visited stations and urged poorly paid Aboriginal workers either to go on strike or to quit and join the movement, which was engaged mainly in mining ventures. A few Jigalong men who had been working on stations north of the mission joined the movement for a short period. In 1959 Pindan members attempted to recruit more workers at Jigalong, but as a result of strong opposition from the missionaries and a dispute between Jigalong and Pindan elders (see Chapter Three), the northerners were unsuccessful (J. Wilson 1961:112). Nevertheless, Jigalong's Aborigines have remained keenly interested in this movement and its effects on traditional cultural elements in the northern area. Because the two areas are linked by cultural transmission, developments in the north can have important effects on what is transmitted and on interarea political relations.

The Aboriginal population at Jigalong increased further during the 1950s as a result of several groups arriving from the desert and of improved health care. Epidemics of measles and influenza caused fewer fatalities as Aboriginal tolerance of alien diseases increased. The population fluctuated during the year mainly as a result of economic factors. The economic pattern that had been evolving was now firmly fixed: most able-bodied men spent much of the year away working on stations. They left behind a relatively stable nucleus of wives, children, old and unemployable people, and a few mission employees. Some station workers took their wives with them; others who were polygynous left one wife at the mission to keep an eye on their children. The seasonal nature of station employment, however, allowed workers to return to the mission periodically throughout the year and for long holidays over Christmas, the midsummer season when most station activities ceased.

In 1960 legislation was passed making all Australian Aborigines eligible for Old Age and Invalid Pensions. At Jigalong this stabilized the residence of most older adults, because if they moved about they would lose income until their pension checks caught up with them. The missionaries who administered the welfare payments used this authority to impress upon the pensioners that if they left the mission they would forego their welfare income.

The mission was particularly concerned to keep the old people and schoolchildren at the settlement because of the nature of its financial support. Its combined income from church sources, stock raising, and the store was insufficient to run the settlement, so the mission relied heavily on state and federal government funding. Apart from grants-in-aid for specific projects, most of this money was allocated on a per capita basis, so the more children and pensioners present, the more government monies received. The mission allotted the pensioners two dollars ($2.25 in United States dollars) a week pocket money and withheld the rest in exchange for the food, clothing, and other items that it issued them. Some of this money went into a building fund, and in 1962 the mission undertook the first construction work in the Camp. Iron huts, latrines, and a water tap were installed, but the buildings were not popular with the Aborigines, most of whom preferred their simpler and more mobile camps.

There were clear indications by about 1960 that the long period of uneasy truce between the adult Aborigines and the missionaries was coming to an end. The Aborigines had tolerated the presence of the missionaries, for in spite of the latter's concerted attempts to convert the schoolchildren and turn them against their parents, no direct attacks had been made on the traditional religious life of the Aboriginal adults. For reasons that are discussed later, the move to Jigalong had intensified this religious life, and the Aborigines were quite willing to ignore the missionaries' bitter opposition to the traditional culture. This mutual awareness of opposition, however, made each party distrust the other.

At one stage a group of adults took thirty children with them and fled the mission, believing rumors that the real reason the missionaries were sending some of the children down to Perth, the state capital, was to circumsize the boys. Circumcision is an operation of central importance in the Aboriginal initiation process, and the rumor (which was false) was readily believed because the Aborigines were well aware of the missionaries' urge to undermine traditional activities. When reporting this incident, the missionaries also alleged that the Aborigines were holding teen-age girls captive in the bush until the men to whom they had been promised in marriage could come to Jigalong and claim them.

The Aborigines were increasingly annoyed at the mission's policy of "protecting" older girls, which consisted of keeping them under close surveillance most of the day and under lock and key at night in their special dormitory. The missionaries wanted to control these girls as long as possible in the hope of converting them and played on the girls' disinclination to be given in marriage to much older men. Both the girls and the missionaries stood to benefit by this situation, but there was one drawback. The older girls shared none of the missionaries' obsessions with the evils of premarital sexual activity and periodically rebelled by breaking out of their dormitory and fleeing into the bush or into Camp, or, as on one memorable occasion, by breaking *into* the boys' dormitory. The mission would be thrown into an uproar as frantic search parties of missionaries, aided by some parents, spent most of the night beating around the bushes. Any girl who subsequently was found to be pregnant suffered an immediate fall from grace and was banished to the Camp. Thus were the high hopes of the missionaries repeatedly dashed.

The period from the early 1960s was marked by a steady deterioration in Aboriginal-missionary relations at Jigalong, with a corresponding intensification of intergroup conflict. The Aborigines, influenced in part by the uniformly negative attitude of their station employers towards the mission, were united in their distrust of the missionaries. They especially disliked the mission superintendent because of his alleged provocations, including the shooting of Camp dogs, censoring the mail, underfeeding pensioners, abducting a girl to prevent her marriage to an older man, inflicting degrading punishments upon wrong-doers, and thrashing children and older girls for misbehavior and crimes such as missing Sunday School. Matters came to a head at the end of 1962. When school ended for the year, the Aborigines took their children and held their annual "big meeting" in the bush away from mission property, leaving only twelve aged Aborigines at the mission. About thirty pensioners and children returned by March, but the remainder moved north to the town of Nullagine. These Aborigines sent their children to school there and even talked of removing their sacred paraphernalia from Jigalong.

The missionaries were understandably panic-stricken. They might lose not only a large amount of government funding, but also their reason for staying on at Jigalong; with no souls to save, they would be lost. Two senior church officials made a special visit to the area, but it was not until the Native Welfare authorities threatened to suspend all ration issues that most Aborigines decided to return with their children to the mission. A few families went north to join the Pindan movement, but within a year all had returned to the Jigalong area.

July 1964 was a high point in the mission's history because in that month the first Christian marriage service was performed for Aborigines. The groom was a Christian Aborigine who had come to the mission years previously to work as a stockman. The bride, a Jigalong girl, had earlier refused to marry a much older man to whom she was promised and was an early convert to the faith. Besides this couple, several teen-age girls regularly took Communion and were professed Apostolics. These are the only successes the mission can claim since its establishment; there have been no male Aborigine converts.

In the period between 1963 and the ethnographic present (the mid-1960s) several more groups of desert Aborigines, totaling seventy persons, have settled at the mission. Most are Mandjildjara-speakers who have come from the vicinity of the Canning Stock Route. These appear to be the last of the desert immigrants, as the area east of Jigalong has no Aborigines.

CHAPTER THREE

The Jigalong Mob

While at the mission, Jigalong Aborigines still identify themselves primarily in terms of their section name (see below) and linguistic group of origin, but whenever they are away from the mission, their primary identification is in terms of the "mob," as they put it, to which they belong. This form of identification is reinforced by the whites' habit of referring to them by their settlement affiliation, but more importantly by the fact that the Aborigines themselves think of Jigalong as their home. The label "Jigalong mob" that the Aborigines give themselves connotes their new form of local organization and indicates their feeling of common identity when contrasting themselves with outsiders.

Social Organization

Demography. Table 3.1 lists available population figures for Jigalong between 1947 and 1970. This table indicates a steadily increasing population and considerable fluctuation in numbers within a given year, caused mainly by the movement of able-bodied men to and from stations. The population is usually largest in midsummer when the demand for station labor is least and most workers return to the mission for the long holiday and to attend "big meetings" there. Visiting groups swell the numbers

Table 3.1

	Adult Male Aborigines	Adult Female Aborigines	Aborigine School-Children	Aborigine Preschool-Children	Whites	Total
1947	31	38		35	8	112
June 1963	26	38	40	13	15	132
Sept. 1963	36	51	54	23	20	184
Dec. 1963	59	76	69	38	20	262
July 1964	56	74	71	32	20	253
Sept. 1964	37	62	65	29	23	216
Dec. 1964	109	101	78	52	17	357
Mar. 1966	79	78	59	25	17	258
July 1966	52	66	44	45	15	222
Aug. 1967	48	77	61	37	18	241
Nov. 1969	113	112	55	77	12	369
Dec. 1969	170	157	81	101	6	515
Jan. 1970	108	105	50	78	7	348

for about a month in December and January, but after they leave
and local men return to work the population decreases considerably.

The July 1964 Aboriginal population (103 males; 130 fe-
males) has been chosen as the basis for the following statistics.
The apparent imbalance in favor of female adults is caused by the
absence of many men who are away on stations. If absentees are
included, the total number of Aborigines belonging to the Jigalong
mob would be closer to 300. Of the adults only 10 percent were
born in the Jigalong area, while 88.5 percent were born in the
desert; whereas only 14.6 percent of the children (under fifteen
years of age) were desert born and 51.5 percent were born either
at the mission or in Port Hedland, where some women are flown for
the birth. The remaining children were born at nearby stations
or towns.

Table 3.2 lists the Jigalong population according to linguistic
group of origin. The "other" category includes Gajadjara, Djar-

Table 3.2

Linguistic Group	Adults	Children	Total	Percentage
Mandjildjara	70	58	128	54.9%
Gaḍudjara	45	37	82	35.2%
Wanman	9	1	10	4.7%
Other	6	7	13	5.2%

gudi, Njijabaḻi, Njaṇumaḍa, Guwara, and Djaṟu people, of whom
most identify with one of the two dominant groups, as do Wanman
people. Map 4 shows the approximate locations of these linguistic
group areas, as well as all other linguistic groups that are identified by Jigalong people. Because of the migrations, place of birth
no longer coincides with linguistic group affiliation. For example,
most children now born at Jigalong, which is in Njijabaḻi territory,
inherit their affiliation from their parents.

From Map 4 it can be seen that the Mandjildjara area is both
the largest and the furthest from the mission. There was a rela-

NOTE: Dotted lines indicate approximate boundaries of linguistic groups in the Jigalong area.

Map 4. Linguistic Group Perspective of Jigalong Aborigines — 1964.

tively large geographic spread of people now identifying themselves as Mandjildjara; this spread is reflected in a larger range of variation and more acceptable alternatives in Mandjildjara vocabulary than in other dialects spoken at the mission. Despite fairly clear distinctions between the two major dialects, they are closely related and mutually intelligible. There is an increasing tendency for young people to speak a composite dialect with the addition of some English words.

The Camp. The camp is usually centered around the pensioners' huts whose fixed foundations tend to disguise the fact that the settlement is still relatively impermanent. It consists of a motley collection of abodes, mostly primitive structures of iron, canvas, bushes, and poles, which are easily realigned to adapt to prevailing weather conditions. These camps are readily moved when the immediate vicinity becomes too dirty, or after a death has occurred. In the latter case, the spirit of the recently deceased

Plate 4. The "main street" at Jigalong (looking south): the two woodchoppers are mission employees.

Plate 5. Jigalong Camp: women having morning tea outside a tent camp.

/person is believed to return to its camp frequently, so everyone vacates the surrounding area for some months after a death.

The main camping area extends for half a mile along the western side of Jigalong Creek, about 200 yards west of the settlement buildings (see Map 3). The general impression is one of ugly disorder, with hordes of underfed dogs scavenging everywhere, and a lot of litter and abandoned vehicles scattered about (cf. Meggitt 1962:75). There are usually broad spatial divisions of camping areas according to linguistic group and area of origin. Groups tend to recreate their precontact orientation toward one another; thus Gaḍudjara camp lies to the west and south of Mandjildjara and other groups from further north. Usually, however, there is no clear demarcation between the two main sets of camps, and often they overlap considerably. Some shelters are built quite close together and sometimes actually adjoin, when the families concerned have close kinship and friendship links. There is a tradition of intermarriage between Mandjildjara and Gaḍudjara families who have been friends for several decades, so many of their children now claim joint affiliation.

The Family and Marriage. A distinctive feature of the family at the mission is the partial separation of school-age children from their parents by the dormitory system. In accordance with state law, all children over six must attend the government school at Jigalong. Parents have the legal right to keep their children with them in Camp, but the missionaries make dormitory living compulsory by threatening sanctions such as withholding rations or police intervention.

If one bears in mind the partial absence of school-age children, the typical family unit is nuclear or composite. It consists of a man, his wife or wives, their older unmarried daughters and sons, with the possible addition of other relatives. The latter may include a married daughter and her children whose husband is away working, an elderly "wife" whom the man looks after, and perhaps his aged mother if she has chosen not to camp with some other widows.

Traditional custom does not restrict the number of wives a man may have, but the number is limited by a man's ability to control and retain them and also by the availability of eligible women. Despite a stated preference by married men for two wives, a sample of forty men revealed only 26.8 percent polygynous marriages, with an average of 1.4 wives per husband. Many contemporary marital conflicts stem from the husband's attempts to take a second wife. Informants claim that polygyny was more common traditionally, and that co-wives usually got along well together.[1]

Infant betrothal is still the ideal and is commonly practiced, but fewer girls now marry the men to whom they were originally betrothed. Whereas the great majority of girls are married before they are nineteen, boys never marry so young because they must complete a substantial portion of their initiation process before even considering marriage.[2] Although some young men now marry in their mid-twenties before they have fully completed their initiation, there are no cases of unsubincised men marrying.

Table 3.3 gives a population breakdown in terms of resident family units and marital status of Aborigines at Jigalong. There are actually 71 schoolchildren in the dormitories; the six unaccounted for in the table are children whose fathers *and* mothers were absent from the mission at the time of the census. The residential family unit averages 4.5 members (including dormitory children).

The asterisks in the table denote people with absent or "divorced" spouses. Divorce, which is uncommon at Jigalong, occurs when a man publicly relinquishes his claims to his wife. Women cannot initiate this step, but by elopement may eventually accomplish the same end. Older divorced women and widows of the same linguistic group tend to camp together; they are sometimes joined by women of the co-wife category who are temporarily

---

[1] Traditionally, there were good economic reasons why an older first wife should welcome a young, strong girl into the family as second wife, especially in view of the great importance of gathering activities to the family's diet. The age difference between the two women was usually considerable, and the younger one was in an acknowledged position of subordination to the senior wife.

[2] Traditionally, as now, boys were circumcised between the ages of about sixteen and eighteen, and were subincised about a year later. At circumcision, one of the boy's initiators, a "MB," would promise as wife one of his own or his brothers' small daughters. If all went well in the interim, and gifts had been exchanged between the families concerned, the girl would be sent to live with her husband before puberty. By that time the husband would be in his late twenties. There was no marriage ceremony.

Table 3.3

	Adults		Dependents	
	Males	Females	Preschool-Children	Schoolchildren in Dormitories
41 full family units	41	57	30	57
Widows		9		3
Unattached women*		3		3
Unmarried girls (Dormitory)		4		
Unmarried girls (Camp)		1	1	
Widowers	2		1	2
Unmarried men	11			
Unattached men*	2			
Total Population	56	74	32	65

camping apart from their husbands — as the result of an argument or perhaps during their menstrual period. Young unmarried men usually camp together, regardless of linguistic group affiliation, but eat meals with parents or other close relatives such as grandparents or married siblings. A few divorced or widowed men prefer to camp by themselves much of the time, often close to a "mother" with whom they eat meals. A few men camp near a "wife" who sometimes feeds them and acts periodically as a sexual partner. The permanency of such arrangements, which at times could be considered polyandrous, depends mainly on the attitude of the husband concerned. At Jigalong there are two long-term arrangements of this type, each involving one woman and two men.

Although it is constantly impinged upon by the wider kinship system and the communal atmosphere of the Camp, the family is the basic kin group and social unit. Admittedly, it has lost some of its traditional economic self-sufficiency; its school-age children are fed, clothed, and sheltered by the mission, and its members who are pensioners or employed locally are also fed and clothed by the mission. But family members spend much time together and usually interact more intensively with one another than with other relatives. The unit plays a central role in the early socialization of its children by providing their main source of affection and security. It does not, however, monopolize these functions. Children are always interacting with older relatives who lavish much attention and affection on them and impart awareness of traditional values. The children are given a great deal of freedom, and adults seldom punish or even chastise them.

The attitudes of the parent-relative-peer socializers contrast sharply with those of the schoolteachers and missionaries. The teachers attempt to inculcate some of the wider society's middle-class values and behavior patterns, and the missionaries supplement this secular teaching with lessons in Apostolic Christianity. Two conflicting sets of pressures are thus at work on the Aboriginal children. It is clear, though, that the influence of the Camp proves the more powerful in the long term; the children are growing up more tradition-oriented than white-oriented in their general outlook and behavior.

The Kinship System. While it is generally agreed that all Australian Aboriginal kinship systems share an underlying homogeneity, anthropologists have divided them into five key types as an aid to understanding how they work (see Elkin 1954:49-79 or R. and C. Berndt 1964:69-81 for summaries). The kinship system possessed by Jigalong Aborigines combines elements of two key types, the Kariera and Aluridja, named for groups found near the northwest and southeast extremities of the Western Desert.

At Jigalong, marriage is permitted with either cross-cousin ("MBD" or "FZD" in the case of a male Ego), and among both groups a section system operates (see below), as in the Kariera system.[3] Aluridja elements include the existence of only two terms in the grandparent and grandchild generations (one term for FF, MF, SS, DS and one for FM, MM, SD, DD) and the classification

---

[3] When citing kinship terms, I use standard abbreviations, with the symbol Z used to distinguish "sister" from S "son"; for example, FZS would be father's sister's son. Classificatory relationships are distinguished from consanguineal relationships by the use of double quotation marks to enclose them, thus: "FZ."

of some cross-cousins as siblings ("B" and "Z"), who are therefore nonmarriageable.[4]

Although the kin terminology used at Jigalong does not distinguish between actual and classificatory relatives, the differences are recognized and are evidenced in a varying intensity of feeling, which depends on the closeness of the particular kinship link involved.[5] All Jigalong Aborigines consider one another relatives, and they order their relationships and their appropriate behavior patterns towards each other through the operation of the kinship system.

People prefer to address each other by kin term rather than by name, so kinship terms are in constant daily use.[6] Most terminology reflects the existence of generation levels, in that members of the same grouping (which includes grandparent and grandchild generations in addition to siblings, spouses, cousins, and siblings-in-law) use identical reciprocal terms in most cases, which express the openness and high degree of equality in their relationships.[7] On the other hand, people in adjacent level groupings (all members of the first ascending and descending generations) are usually addressed by a non-identical reciprocal term, which indicates that there is a difference in status between the two people concerned. For example, a person and his or her grandchildren address each other by reciprocal terms that vary only according to the sex of

---

[4] The kinship terminology at Jigalong resembles most closely that of certain Aluridja groups, particularly the Kokata (Elkin 1954:73). I therefore suspect that the desert ancestors of the Jigalong people originally possessed an Aluridja-type kinship system, and that this was later modified by their adoption of the four section system. This modification caused the original system to take on some of the appearance of a Kariera-type system.

[5] Readers who have no prior knowledge of how classificatory kinship systems work should consult a general anthropology text or a kinship analysis manual such as that by Schusky (1972).

[6] Although all linguistic groups at the mission share the same general kinship system, there are differences in nomenclature, and a distinction exists between Mandjildjara and Gaḍudjara interpretations of certain marriage rules; but these cause the people no difficulties.

[7] An exception here would be the terminological distinction made between older and younger siblings, which reflects the fact that in general, younger siblings are subordinate to older.

the person being addressed; e.g. "SS" and "DS" are *njamu*, "SD" and "DD" are *njami* when Ego addresses them. But a person addressing his or her parents or children uses non-identical reciprocal terms; e.g. the reciprocal of *mama* "F" and *jaguḍi* "M" is *gadja* "S" or *jundal* "D."[8]

Ideally a man must choose his wife from the category of women he calls by the term for "spouse"; these women will be members of the classificatory cross-cousin category. Marriage with an actual or consanguineally close cross-cousin is rare at Jigalong. The existence of nonmarriageable classificatory cross-cousins and the common practice of *naraṇmaridi*, the "splitting up" of certain "spouses" and "siblings-in-law" so that henceforth they are termed "sibling" and are treated as such, have still not been explained adequately.[9]

"Wrong" marriages, defined as unions between two people who do not call each other by the term for "spouse," are uncommon at Jigalong, and this is a good indication of the present strength of traditional kinship arrangements. Only three couples are wrongly married and have persisted in their relationship despite strong community opposition in the initial stages. In each case the kinship relationship involved is "MB"-"ZD," and the couple concerned had been lovers for years before actually living together. This supports the observation that casual sexual liaisons between people so related are not condemned to the extent that other irregular liaisons are. None of the couples has children, which saves the community the embarrassing problem of determining the section membership of their offspring.

One possible reason for the low incidence of wrong marriage at Jigalong is that the kinship system allows a person a wider choice within the category of "spouse" than, for instance, in systems where all cross-cousins are classified as siblings. There is greater choice, too, in terms of actual numbers of potential

---

[8] The term *umaṛi*, which denotes the male Ego-"WM" relationship, is an exception, but it is never used as a term of address because people so related must strictly avoid each other.

[9] This problem is complicated by the number of factors involved and by the high degree of arbitrariness in a person's decision to classify some others as "sibling" rather than "spouse" or "WB" (cf. Tonkinson 1966:118-122).

spouses, now that groups from different areas of the desert are congregated in one place.

Kin Behavioral Patterns. Each kinship term connotes a particular pattern of expected behavior. Aborigines avoid contact with people to whom their specific kinship relationship is not known, until formal introductions take place. When the kinship links are ascertained, confidence replaces embarrassment because the Aborigines concerned know their expected mutual behavior and interact accordingly.

These kin behavioral patterns can be viewed as a continuum, with joking and avoidance relationships at opposite extremes. In all cases, however, people differ in conforming to the behavioral norm, invariably in the direction of lessened restraint. This partial relaxation usually occurs between people who are of similar age and sex and have been close friends since childhood; their interation retains most of its openness, regardless of their particular kin relationship. Both joking relationships, with their sexual horseplay, and avoidance relationships, where people make sudden changes of direction to give someone a wide berth (anything closer than about thirty feet is considered a near miss), are readily discernible in the Camp situation. But other kin behavioral patterns, such as restraint relationships, are less evident because they are defined negatively. For example, a man and his actual parents, siblings, adult children, wife's brothers, and his classificatory mothers and daughters should not touch, joke, pass food or other objects hand to hand, or talk more than minimally and formally.

Relationships among women are generally less restrained than those among men; a woman may talk freely and openly with most other women, whereas a man may do so only with certain categories of male relatives. Also, adult-child interaction differs greatly from that between most adults; children behave unrestrainedly towards all adults, regardless of kin categories concerned, until they reach their early teens. The interaction of adult males with most close consanguineal kin is generally restrained; even between full or half brothers there is partial avoidance and restricted interaction, which is not a common feature of Aboriginal culture (Elkin 1954:121).

The Section System and Other Groupings. The Aborigines of Jigalong come from areas that traditionally possessed a section system, in which everyone is born a member of one of four named groups, or sections. [10]   The sections are exogamous, and although they indicate intermarrying divisions, they are not of themselves sufficient to regulate marriage, which operates through rules expressed in terms of kinship categories. [11]   It is important to realize that sections never operate as discrete entities in everyday life but are useful principally as convenient reference terms or labels; people frequently refer to others using section terminology rather than personal names. [12]

   The following diagram shows the arrangement of the sections at Jigalong; the symbol $=$ connects intermarrying sections, and the arrows indicate the direction in which descent is traced and connect the sections of a mother and her children.

$$\begin{array}{l} \rightarrow \text{BANAGA} = \text{GAR̩IMARA} \leftarrow \\ \rightarrow \text{BUR̩UɳU} = \text{MILAɳGA} \leftarrow \end{array}$$

The same section name is used for its members of both sexes. The system works as follows: taking a Banaga male as our starting point, he marries one or more members of the Gar̩imara section whom he calls "spouse." He cannot marry *any* Gar̩imara woman, because some other female relatives, such as his real and classificatory FM and DD, are also members of the Gar̩imara section. The children of his marriage will belong to the Milaṇga section and will, when they grow up, take their spouses from the Bur̩uṇu sec-

---

[10] A few of the more recent desert immigrants used subsection system terminology (division into eight categories with separate male and female terms in each; cf. Meggitt 1962:61), but this caused no problems at Jigalong; local Aborigines are aware of the subsection system and know which subsection pairs correspond to which section, so the newcomers were immediately put into the appropriate section.

[11] Misconceptions about subsections and sections abound in anthropological literature, where they are frequently and erroneously referred to as "marriage classes" and are discussed as if each existed as a corporate group. For example, "A(n Aboriginal Australian) marriage class is more than a matrimonial unit, it is a kind of club." (Coon 1971:214)

[12] Aborigines are usually most reluctant to reveal either their own or anyone else's personal name. One's name is as much a part of one's self as are parts of the body. A sorcerer could thus use a person's name to work sorcery against him.

tion. Children of Milaṇga women will be Gaṛimara, and of Milaṇga men will be Banaga. This system results in the grouping of certain sets of relatives in each section, as indicated by the diagram below, which uses a male Ego in Section A as starting point:

A *Ego*; B; Z;
   FF; MM;
   MMB; WMF;
   SS; SD; etc.

B W; WB;
   BW; ZH; MF; FM;
   MBD; MBS; FZD;
   FZS; ZSD; ZSS; etc.

C M; MB; WF;
   SW; DH;
   ZD; ZS;
   FMBD; FMBS; etc.

D F; FZ; WM;
   S; D;
   ZDH; ZSW;
   MMBD; MMBS; etc.

The section system thus crosscuts the kinship system, embraces the entire Jigalong population, and is shared by neighboring Aboriginal groups. Even the Camp dogs possess section membership, matrilineally inherited, and are addressed frequently by section name, or else by given name or kinship term. Babies are usually called by section names until personal names are chosen. Although specific kinship links determine largely the nature of interpersonal behavior, reference to sections is useful as a general guide to behavior. For example, a Banaga man approaching a group of women needs to know only that there are Milaṇga in that group to alert him to the possible presence of "WM," whom he must carefully avoid. Once an Aborigine knows the section membership of an incoming stranger, he can immediately reduce the possibilities of their classificatory kinship link. For instance, a Banaga man, on learning that the stranger is Gaṛimara, knows that the latter could be his "WB," "MF," "ZSS," or "cross cousin." Once their classificatory kinship link has been determined by discussions between local elders and the stranger and a formal introduction has taken place, they can interact with assurance.

Although sections can be used to summarize social relationships, this method is often ambiguous. Meggitt makes this point in reference to the Walbiri, whose culture is similar to that of the Western Desert peoples, and adds:

When important questions arise concerning, for instance, the disposal of a woman in marriage, the selection of a circumcizer, the avenging of

a death, or the organization of a revelatory ceremony, specific genealogical connections and local community affiliations constitute the approved frame of reference within which decisions are made (1962:169).

This observation applies equally well to Jigalong, where under
most circumstances the section membership of the principals concerned is of secondary importance because it is too broad a method of classification.

Inherent in any section system are three dual grouping possibilities: patrilineal moieties, matrilineal moieties, and adjacent or
alternating generation levels, all of which are diagrammed below:

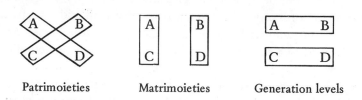

Patrimoieties   Matrimoieties   Generation levels

Neither of the first two kinds of grouping operates at Jigalong, and
there is no evidence that they existed traditionally as corporate
groups or social entities of any kind. Alternating generation level
groupings, however, do occur. A person refers to all members of
his or her own generation level group (i.e. real and classificatory
B, Z, MM, MF, FF, FM, BW, ZH, MBS, MBD, FZS, FZD, etc.) as
maṟira and those of the adjacent generation level group (all kin in
the first ascendant and first descendant generations; F, M, S, D,
etc.) as *jinara*. For example, a Banaga person would call all other
Banaga and Gaṟimara *maṟira* "own group," and all Buṟuṇu and
Milaṇga *jinara* "other group," whereas a Buṟuṇu person would call
all other Buṟuṇu and Milaṇga *maṟira* and all Banaga and Gaṟimara
jinara. This division of the community into two groups is not important in mundane affairs but is a common feature of religious
activities. For many rituals, seating arrangements are made on
this basis, and the proceedings invariably include the frequent expression of ritual opposition between the two groups so formed.

Another kind of dual grouping, similar to the alternating general level groupings, is also important in the religious life at Jigalong, particularly those aspects that concern male initiation.
Members of the *djindjanuṇu* group (mostly "own side" generation
level members, but minus all close consanguineal relatives, "sib-

lings" of both sexes, and some "cross cousins" of the initiate, who side with the other group) are active in the organization and execution of the ritual proceedings. Members of the larger *ga:ngu* group ("other side" generation level members plus those listed above) make the preliminary plans and raise the necessary food for the feasts that accompany the ritual activities, but take little active part, except for lying down and wailing, in the rituals.

Change and Continuity in Social Organization. As a result of their shift to a sedentary existence at the mission, the Aborigines abandoned their traditional local group organization; the disappearance of the horde and local group is the most obvious change in their social organization. The new community consists of the remnants of many different local groups from widely separated homelands, and with the possible exception of linguistic groups (reflected to a certain extent in their camping arrangements), their earlier groups are no longer evident in any physical sense. However, close ties of friendship and kinship continue to bind some families who were members of the same local group traditionally, even after several decades of life at Jigalong.

In terms of obvious continuities with the past, both the section and kinship systems are functioning strongly, with little modification as a result of the altered environment. No major signs of incipient breakdown have appeared. This situation contrasts somewhat with several of the more acculturated neighboring communities where Western influences have been stronger; many wrong marriages, including some that involve uninitiated males, have occurred, and most kin behavioral patterns, especially those of avoidance, have been relaxed or abandoned.

Economics

Station Employment. Aborigines in greatest demand for station work are young men skilled at riding horses and motorcycles who can find jobs as stockmen for most of the year if they desire. Some middle-aged men who have developed skills, such as fence-making, windmill maintenance, and stock work, can find work at intervals during the year, as can men who work as general laborers. Many of their wives, too, may work as domestics while on the same stations. Most stations in the marginal Jigalong area cannot afford to employ more than a few Aborigines as a permanent labor force, and even these employees are let go in midsummer. Graziers who need labor recruit from the mission or towns, where Aborigines spend time between jobs. Wages vary from about four to twenty dollars per week, with clothes, tobacco, and sometimes meals deducted from this sum. When the job is completed, employees are paid by check and return either to town or to the mission. Meekatharra and Wiluna are the towns usually chosen by Jigalong people, because they have relatives and a place to camp in both.

The Aboriginal work force of most stations varies, with the exception of a few "permanent" employees, and follows no set pattern of linguistic group affiliation. Aborigines try not to be in the same work force as those with whom they have avoidance relationships. When they can choose their workmates, they opt for close friends, but kin ties are thus implied since a person's friends conventionally come from categories of relatives towards whom he can behave with a lack of restraint.

The money which may accumulate while they are working rarely lasts long once the Aborigines hit town or return to the mission. Their earnings are quickly depleted by gifts to relatives, gambling, and sometimes drinking in town. Thrift is a value that has no place in Aboriginal society, which emphasizes instead sharing and unselfishness as primary virtues. The individual is enmeshed in a community-wide net of obligations and responsibilities to many relatives, with whom he is expected to share his wealth and thus enhance his reputation as a "good" man. Some of the more permanent station employees do manage to save sums amounting to several hundred dollars which they use to buy second-hand vehicles, but they are never criticized for this because they are unselfish in their use of the vehicles to aid friends and relatives.

It is impossible to calculate exactly how much of the money earned on stations later reaches the mission, because it arrives with returning workers and in mail that some send home, but I doubt that it would exceed three thousand dollars annually. The half-dozen or so workers who own vehicles spend considerable sums on gas and spare parts. These vehicles are mostly old, battered, and unreliable, but the Aborigines who own them have become

skilled amateur mechanics and are particularly adept at "canni-
balizing" parts from abandoned wrecks. These few vehicles see
heavy service while they last and are valued by the Aborigines for
the added mobility they afford.

Mission Employment. Since most middle-aged and older Jigalong Aborigines lack the necessary skills to gain employment on
stations, they form the nucleus of the settlement's adult population, on which the mission relies heavily for its continuing operation.
The male work force is not large; there is one permanent stockman,
assisted by two youths, several laborers who are employed on a
semipermanent basis, and about ten men who work as woodchoppers. The latter work for food rations and clothing; the
others work for wages of four to five dollars per week, plus food
rations and clothing, but do not usually receive cash because they
have accounts at the mission store and take their wages in kind.

About thirty five women comprise the female labor force
and are employed as laundresses, kitchen workers, hospital aides,
and housegirls. Two days a week the laundresses wash the dormitory and hospital laundry, in return for meals and clothing. The
other female workers receive food, clothing, and two dollars per
month wages. Thus the mission has a good supply of cheap labor,
which enables it to run the dormitory system and provide daily
meals for the pensioners, schoolchildren, and work force. The
composition of this work force varies, as there are always substi-
tutes available for sick or absent workers. The work is rarely arduous, the Aborigines can proceed at their own pace, and it occasions a great deal of sociability among workers.

Other Income. Aboriginal pensioners receive two cooked
meals a day, periodic issues of clothing and bedding, and two dollars per week pocket money. The cash is exchanged for food at
the mission store almost immediately after it is given. Since the
rest of their pensions is withheld by the mission for various purposes, very little of the income from government sources circulates
in the Camp.

Few other sources of income exist at Jigalong. Some station
workers and relatives living in town areas mail small sums to close
relatives at the mission from time to time. A few men earn small
sums of money periodically from the sale of weapons they make,
and some who go hunting for dingoes earn a small government

bounty for each scalp turned in. [13]   Most of the money that appears in the Camp is earned on stations and brought back by employees. Much of it circulates through gift-giving and gambling,
but sooner or later it ends up in the mission store because there is
nowhere else nearby to spend it. Some money is always given to
people making brief trips to town, for the purchase of tobacco
and cigarettes which are not stocked at the mission store.

   Consumption Patterns. Jigalong Aborigines spend very little
money on durable articles outside a fairly narrow range of things
they have come to regard as necessities. Items such as knives, axes,
razor blades, plastic buckets, billycans (in which tea is brewed),
blankets, canvas sheets, files, chisels, matches, flashlights and bat-
teries, water-bags, soap, and hair oil are steady sellers at the mission store. Tobacco, which was chewed traditionally and is craved
by the Aborigines, is always in demand and in short supply. Apart
from articles of clothing, almost all other purchases are foodstuffs,
mainly flour, tea, sugar, salt, canned meats, milk, fruits and jam,
cookies and candy — and fresh meat, fruits, and vegetables when
they are available. In town, most adult Aborigines supplement
their diet with beer and wine. The only more expensive items that
attract the attention of male Aborigines are rifles and secondhand
vehicles. A few of the young adults own portable radios and guitars. Young adults tend to spend the most money on clothing and
items of personal adornment. Emulation of the "cowboy" image
is every young man's aim, so broad buckles, big hats, riding boots,
and tight blue jeans are popular. Cowboy comics, movies, and
country and western music are also popular with younger people.

   Subsistence Activities. In both the mission and station environments, hunting and food gathering are no longer matters of
necessity for the Aborigines, yet these activities remain popular.
Most older people have not lost the skills of the desert, and they
greatly enjoy the opportunity to get away from the constant noise
and the large numbers of people in the Camp. They are also
prompted by a strong desire to vary and augment their diet. They
all love meat, and large pieces of kangaroo or emu are always pre-

---

[13] The dingo, a semidomesticated dog, was brought to Australia by Aborigines but was not normally used as a source of food. For a good discussion
of the place of the dingo in Aboriginal culture, see Meggitt (1965).

ferable to small ration-size portions of mutton. In certain seasons, women dig large quantities of yam and flax-lily bulbs and gather grass seeds and wild fruit, but food gathering is now secondary to meat getting.

Groups of men sometimes hunt game in order to fulfill ritual commitments, especially during "big meetings." At such times the mission population is greatly enlarged by visiting groups, and money is often in short supply, so hunting provides much-needed protein. Men and women often hunt on foot, with specially trained dogs, but much hunting is done by groups of men who use vehicles and rifles. Such forays by vehicles are generally brief, lasting only a few hours. People who hunt on foot often camp out for a night or two over weekends, and in the cool midwinter season small groups may go on longer trips into the desert. On these trips, which may last from one to three weeks, Aborigines also hunt for wild dingoes and gather the special saplings from which excellent spears are made.

The local people engage in few other traditional economic pursuits. Men still spend considerable time making weapons, mainly spears, spear-throwers, boomerangs, and clubs, which are mostly for personal use. The community does not permit the use of nontraditional weapons during fights. Some older men and women spin human hair and make hair-belts, but this, like the carving of sacred wooden boards, belongs in the realm of ritual rather than economic activity.

Leisure Activities. As in the days when they were living off the land, the Aborigines have ample leisure time, even if they work as mission employees. Household tasks such as wood-gathering, cooking, altering or relocating one's camp, and water-carting occupy relatively little time, so people can do as they please most of the day.

Visiting and gossiping are favored adult pastimes. Since many people simply wander about, the composition of any given group is rarely static for long. Men wander more frequently than women, who tend to group more consistently according to particular friendships and kin ties. Groups of women stay together longer than men also (except when the latter are meeting to discuss ritual matters) because they often work at something, such as washing or sewing, while they chat. Adults and older siblings spend much time caring for and playing with small children and babies. Most people take an early afternoon siesta, especially during the hot season. They rise about dawn and unless there is ritual activity in progress, they usually bed down for the night two or three hours after sunset.

Some younger and middle-aged adults frequently play cards in their spare time. The gamblers, often in mixed sex groups, play poker and "nineup" (a form of baccarat) for money, clothing, tobacco, or other objects. Such activity rarely involves more than about two groups and ten or fifteen people. Often no cards are played until an impetus is provided by the arrival of station workers with money. The Aborigines gamble for the excitement of it rather than the hope of winning a lot. This view is supported by the fact that players never seem to quit while they are ahead.

Initiated men spend much time discussing and participating in activities related to the religious life, which is of central concern to them and is seen as benefiting the entire community. Many meetings, formal and informal, are held in or near Camp to discuss a wide variety of topics concerning current, projected, or past rituals, "big meetings," and religious lore. Many different sacred objects are often displayed, passed around, and commented on by those present. Religious matters are never far from the minds of the men. Although the women are much less preoccupied with ritual concerns, they and the children attend and participate in many rituals held in the Camp area.

Most of the children at Jigalong must attend school six hours a day, five days a week and perform daily chores in and around their dormitories, but this still leaves ample spare time which they divide between the Camp area and the mission. In the Camp, the elders make few demands upon them, so they play games or help amuse younger siblings. The preschoolers are the most leisured class, for they roam the Camp area unchallenged for much of the day. Even their periodic attempts to imitate the sexual activities of their elders are viewed by the latter with lighthearted indifference and do not provoke adult interference.

Politics

Settlement Administration. Jigalong is the Apostolic Church's only Australian mission. Responsibility for the day-to-

day management of the settlement as mission and pastoral enterprise rests with the superintendent, but most important decisions
affecting mission administration are made at the church head-
quarters in Melbourne by Mission Board members, many of whom
have never visited Jigalong. The board recruits missionaries from
its church membership, pays them wages while they are at Jigalong, and allows them one month annual furlough.

As was pointed out earlier, the mission is not financially well-
endowed from church sources and therefore relies heavily on financial aid from both state and federal governments, which demand
some account of money spent. Thus, in addition to answering to
his church superiors in Melbourne, the superintendent must deal
with local representatives of the Native Welfare Department and
with other state and federal officials who make periodic inspec-
tions. The nearest Native Welfare district agency is at Marble Bar,
200 miles north, and the nearest police station is at Nullagine, 140
miles north. The Nullagine policeman makes periodic trips to the
mission to take offenders away for trial and possible imprisonment.

Aboriginal Leadership and Authority. Local Aborigines have
no representation on any advisory or supervisory body involved
with administering the mission. They play no part in the decision-
making processes that relate to their welfare, since neither missionaries nor government officials are in the habit of conferring with
them. There is, however, a "boss" for each of the two main linguistic groups in the Camp. The missionaries sometimes relay in-
structions or information to the Camp via these two men, who also
act as spokesmen for the Aborigines in dealing with the missionaries or visiting whites. Both men work on stations much of the
year, however, and although they are sometimes quite vocal in
Camp meetings, neither enjoys extra status because of his role as
spokesman for the community.

Within the broad constraints of the contact situation, the
Aborigines are largely free to run their internal affairs with a minimum of direct interference from outside agencies. There is a great
deal of self-regulation in the functioning of everyday life, but
when internal problems arise, they are dealt with by the traditional
informal council of initiated men. The council, an ad hoc gathering of whichever initiated men happen to be present on the mission at the time, deals mostly with religious matters, but its mem-

bers may also call public meetings for the adult community at
large to discuss secular topics, especially grievances. The meeting
continues until a unanimous decision is reached (in the sense that
those with objections finally cease to voice them publicly). The
individuals involved generally agree to abide by the decision of the
meeting. Offenders face public denigration and possible physical
punishment such as a beating or several spear wounds in the thigh.
Only rarely, in persistent cases, do council members threaten to
seek outside assistance.

In the traditional culture, authority was largely a function of
sex and age, with the middle-aged and older males wielding the
greatest influence, yet submitting to the will of the council in public affairs. Leadership and authority, in the sense of individuals
telling others to do things, were confined largely to religious
contexts and were always defined situationally. Thus, for each
ritual there were a few men who by virtue of their "ownership,"
or mastery of it, were the acknowledged leaders and directed its
performance. In a different ritual, these men would be fol-
lowers, and another group of "bosses" would take over as leaders.
In the secular life, there was no leadership structure outside the
family, whose male head was its acknowledged leader. Kinship
considerations were always paramount in deciding which action to
initiate with what people. As Meggitt notes, secular leaders were
not needed, since the norms of the religious and kinship systems
constituted an enduring master plan, which met most contingen-
cies and to which there were few approved alternatives (1962:
247). [14]

The use of the two Camp "bosses" for some dealings with
whites is the only concession to change in traditional leadership at
Jigalong. The Aborigines are well aware that "the Government"
is the dominant political force in the country, but their isolation
and the policy of laissez-faire adopted towards them by whites
allow them to feel a sense of autonomy.

---

[14] This view has been recently disputed by Strehlow, who contends that
among the Aranda people of the Central Australian desert there were ceremonial leaders whose authority was very powerful and extended into secular
realms (1970:92-140). Strehlow may be right, despite the anecdotal nature
of his evidence, but at Jigalong, Aboriginal leadership structure accords
closely with that of the Walbiri. Furthermore, there is little to suggest that
it was otherwise traditionally.

Intracommunity Relations. Although most local Aborigines identify with one of the two dominant linguistic groups, intracommunity relations and factionalism are not predicated upon such a division. The two groups are now so closely interrelated that any prolonged conflict would be untenable. Intergroup relations in the past, however, were not always so amicable, and a serious dispute in the late 1950s culminated in a major spear fight. The final settlement of this dispute came with the cutting, carving, and exchange of two large sacred wooden boards in accordance with traditional dictates. Board exchange between individuals or groups puts the seal of finality on conflict so that no recurrence is possible between the parties involved.

The intensified social life that has resulted from large numbers of Aborigines settling at one place has brought with it new tensions and conflicts, which occur more frequently than in the desert when groups were scattered most of the year. Interpersonal conflicts, frequently between close relatives, are common and inevitably public affairs, even when purely domestic in origin. Quarrels are loud, sometimes violent, but usually short-lived, because relatives intervene whenever serious injury looks likely. All but the most minor disagreements quickly attract a crowd of interested spectators. Women's club fights, in particular, generate considerable enjoyment, especially among male spectators. Only the preschool children, who generally go on playing with an almost studied air of disinterest, seem to remain unmoved by such hand-to-hand combat.

When it is suspected that a fight is imminent, an air of tense expectancy fills the Camp. Most people seem to enjoy this change from the Camp routine, except when serious clashes occur among large numbers of men. Today, local Aborigines never fight to kill, and in almost all disputes the combatants observe a traditional behavioral code. Most fights, then, follow fairly predictable patterns with a great deal of verbal exchange and threatening postures but minimal bloodshed. In most men's fights, women play a very important role, intervening to hold the men back and prevent them from fitting spears into their throwers. Occasionally things get out of hand, and spears and boomerangs fly in all directions. For the onlooker, judging the flight path of a spinning boomerang in a high wind is a vital survival skill.

Plate 6. Jigalong Camp: a fully armed man passes a pensioner's hut as he returns from a fight.

The Aborigines seem to favor the airing of grievances rather
than a long-term harboring of smoldering resentment, yet they
take care to minimize the possibilities of serious interpersonal injury. However, I should emphasize that the dominant orientation
of their culture is still towards amicability, sharing, kinship solidarity, and peace, and the normal atmosphere at Jigalong reflects
these values rather than those of conflict.

Intercommunity Relations. Jigalong and its neighboring Aboriginal communities are politically independent, yet all are necessary links in the chain of cultural transmission that unites the Western Desert peoples into a postcontact "society" or religious unit
(cf. Berndt 1959:99). As members of this society, Aborigines may
travel widely in the Western Desert area and find hospitality and
assistance if needed. Besides, Aborigines from one community are
generally related consanguineally and affinally to others in neighboring settlements, and many men have close friends in other communities as a result of working together on stations. Members of
several contiguous communities endeavor to congregate at a pre-
arranged site at least once a year for a period of intensive ritual
and social activity. The size and composition of these "big meetings"

depend on factors such as the location and timing of the meeting, weather conditions, the availability and efficiency of transportation, and the current emotional state of intercommunity relationships.

Jigalong's relations with its southern neighbors at Wiluna are friendlier than those with communities to the north, partly because Jigalong Aborigines have more relatives there than in the north; but more importantly, the less amicable relations with the north stem from past attempts by more sophisticated northerners to pressure Jigalong people into changing certain traditional practices. The northern communities at Marble Bar and Port Hedland have had much more intensive contact with whites. Their best educated and most vocal members have long encouraged less acculturated desert Aborigines to abandon many customs in favor of a "new Law" which its proponents consider better suited to their present situation. The failure of the northerners to attract large numbers of Jigalong people to their mining ventures, which was mentioned in the previous chapter, can be attributed largely to the growing ideological rift between the ritual leaders of the two areas. As soon as the Jigalong elders became aware that the northerners were modifying certain traditional practices and were relaxing marriage and kin behavioral rules, they voiced strong objections and informed the northerners that they had no intention of destroying their Law in this way.

The implications of this conflict have been serious, because it has caused a break in the transmission chain along which new rituals and other items flow from area to area around the Western Desert perimeter. The elders at Jigalong are quite reluctant to hand on rituals to people who, they believe, are abandoning their desert heritage in favor of the white man's culture.

Aboriginal-White Relations. As noted previously, the history of Aboriginal-white relations in the Jigalong area has been a relatively peaceful one, and local whites have interfered minimally in Aboriginal internal affairs.

Despite their special status under the provisions of the State Native Welfare Act, Aborigines are expected in theory to obey all the laws of the land. In practice, the Aborigines tend to disregard the many laws that are not policed among tribally oriented Aborigines (bigamy laws, for instance) and have modified certain practices, such as taking girls under sixteen as wives, only when transgression would almost certainly give rise to police action.

Likewise, communally sanctioned punishment, such as death by spearing, is no longer practiced because the police and courts do not tolerate this usurpation of their powers. Because it is difficult to conceal serious conflicts and the resulting wounds if they occur, Aboriginal men are sometimes jailed after the missionaries report them to the police. The Aborigines dislike police intervention, especially the shooting of Camp dogs as a population control measure, undertaken again at the request of the missionaries. The arrival of the policeman at one end of the Camp usually coincides with a hasty exodus of Aborigines leading their excess dogs to the safety of the bush some distance from the opposite end of Camp.

The missionaries have certain legal administrative powers over the Aborigines, vested in them by the Native Welfare Department, the ultimate legal guardian of Aboriginal interests. But they do not normally interfere in the internal politics of the Aboriginal community unless a crisis, such as a serious fight, attracts their attention. The missionaries are aware of the Aborigines' strong opposition to outside interference, and the conflict-orientation that characterizes interracial relationships on the mission (discussed in Chapter Six) is such that the missionaries tend to keep out of Camp affairs for fear of further conflict and a possible exodus of Aborigines from the mission.

In their relations with other whites, the Aborigines usually adopt a wait-and-see attitude and judge them on an individual basis according to the outcome of their interaction. The Aborigines have not yet developed a generalized feeling of being exploited by whites and do not see themselves as victims of racial prejudice. The Aborigines may acknowledge the technological and political dominance of the whites, but they harbor no feelings of cultural inferiority and retain great pride in their Aboriginal identity and in their traditional culture. In later chapters these strengths are shown to be crucial factors in the Aborigines' struggle against threatening acculturative pressures.

CHAPTER FOUR

The Religious Life

The Australian Aborigines' social organization, and in particular their kinship system, was a major integrating force in their traditional culture. Yet even kinship was overshadowed by the unifying power of the religious life, which underlies and validates the entire culture. The Aborigines of Jigalong still feel that their religion is fundamental to their continued well-being, and they have actively protected it from alien influences. They have been aided in this endeavor by the whites' ignorance of Aboriginal cosmology and by the whites' disinclination to interfere actively with Aboriginal rituals. As a result, the traditional religious life flourishes at Jigalong despite the missionary presence. The Aborigines are self-consciously tradition-oriented in their kinship system, religious life, and core values, because they observe what is happening to their more acculturated Aboriginal neighbors in the towns. Their obvious conclusion is that those who abandon tradition and follow the way of the whites will not survive long as Aborigines; they will "die inside" even though their bodies may live on.

The Dreamtime, The Law, and Mythology

Basic to their notion of religion is the Aborigines' universal belief in the reality of the Dreamtime, the creative period — an indefinable past era when Australia was inhabited only by *djugu-*

ḏani, ancestral beings, and maḷbu, malevolent spirits.[1]   The ancestral beings were part-human, part-animal, and they roamed
about, creating natural features by means of superhuman magical powers as they traveled.   They left the first Aborigines behind at various points along their routes and gave them their
social organization and ground rules for living.   Although they
were guilty of some reprehensible excesses, such as killings and
indiscriminate copulation, the ancestral beings told man to ignore such bad behavior and obey only the master design for life
that was their legacy.[2]

Upon completion of their Dreamtime adventures, the ancestral beings metamorphosed into natural features or heavenly
bodies, in which their life-essence or spirit remains forever.
Since none of them actually died during the conflicts of the creative period, the Dreamtime is timeless and remains relevant to
the present.   The ancestral beings retain their interest in man's
affairs as long as he follows their directives and perpetuates their
founding design.   The ancestors and their associated spirits still
control plant, animal, and human fertility, and their ways must
be followed if this fertility is to be maintained.

Everywhere in the Western Desert, the Aborigines refer to
their heritage from the Dreamtime as "the Law" (defined in
Footnote 3, Chapter One), a concept so central and so pervasive
as to be virtually synonymous with "traditional culture."   The
Aborigines at Jigalong repeatedly stress the necessity of "holding
onto the Law," and in assessing one another's behavior they
commonly use the criterion of whether actions are juḷubiḏinga
'according to the Law.'

The events of the Dreamtime are embodied in songs and
myths, the greatest knowledge of which is concentrated in
the hands of initiated men.   Each desert group that migrated
to Jigalong brought a body of religious knowledge that was

---

[1] For an excellent description of the Dreamtime concept, see Stanner (1958:
158-167).   He has also written with much insight on the nature and structure
of Aboriginal religion (1965a:207-237; 1966).

[2] The relationship between Aboriginal religion and morality is discussed by
R. Berndt, in the context of a Western Desert myth-ritual complex, the
Dinari, which is well known to the Jigalong Aborigines (1970:216-247).

unique in some of its content but not radically different from that of any other group. One of the major consequences of their aggregation at the mission has been a widening of the individual Aborigine's religious knowledge to a far greater extent than would have occurred during the normal course of intergroup cultural transmission.

The Aborigines associate a host of natural features with the ancestral being or beings who are said to have created them, and for these people the physical environment provides concrete proof of the absolute truths embodied in their myths and song-lines.[3] Inevitably, there is some variation in their oral tradition, especially in the realm of mythology, yet the Aborigines share a complete acceptance of the truth of the events and dramas depicted in their myths and songs. They are not doubters and are not given to philosophical speculation about the characters or motives of ancestral beings. If an observer asks Aborigines why they do a particular thing, they will usually answer, "Because it's the Law" or "Because it was done like that in the Dream-time." Further inquiries about why the ancestral beings did it that way in the Dreamtime are always answered with, "We don't know" or "They just did it that way, that's all." The Aborigines never question their religion because they regard the grand design-plan as immutable. Their ideology emphasizes continuity, and change is welcomed only if, as Stanner notes, it fits the forms of permanence (1966:168).

The Aborigines believe that the Western Desert was criss-crossed by a tremendous amount of Dreamtime traffic. An individual knows best the myths and songs involving sites in his home territory. Of the major beings that traveled extensively, an Aborigine will be most familiar with the parts of the myth and songline concerning their exploits in his home area. Such major ancestral beings, known to Aborigines everywhere in the Western Desert, include Wadi Gudjara, Two Men, who are believed to have laid the foundations for much of the Law; Malu,

---

[3] A songline is a series of songs, each consisting of only a few words, which pertains to the travels and exploits of Dreamtime beings. These songs are usually sung in accompaniment to ritual activity, particularly dancing. The Aborigines use the English word "line" frequently to refer to a ritual complex as well as to a song series.

Kangaroo-man; the Minjiburu women who were pursued east-
wards by the rapacious Njiru, famed for his huge penis; Wajuda
the possum people and Gingilba the native cat mob; Djandu the
dogs; Gunagalju the snakes, and a host of others.[4]

Western Desert Aborigines attribute their cultural homogeneity to the fact that the ancestral beings roamed over wide areas
and frequently came into contact with one another. During
such meetings they exchanged sacred and nonsacred objects,
songlines, rituals, and decorations, thus spreading these cultural
elements to the extremes of the desert and beyond. But cultural variation, too, is often explained by certain myths. For
instance, coastal peoples such as the Ŋala do not practice circumcision because, according to the Jigalong Aborigines, the
Two Men tried to do so during the Dreamtime but found that
Ŋala foreskins were too tough to cut.

Besides their great magical powers, which included the
ability to assume their animal form at will, all ancestral beings
carried much paraphernalia, including carved wooden boards
and other sacred objects, which they left behind in the various
places they camped so that man would ultimately discover
them and draw strength and a sense of security from them.[5]
The creative beings also wore elaborate body decorations and
instituted new songs and rituals as they went, usually at some
significant natural feature which they created, such as a waterhole or a big hill. At such sacred sites they created storehouses
of sacred objects (often hidden in caves), so that man would
emulate them and would always respect these sites as sacred.

---

[4] For descriptions of Western Desert mythological beings see: R. and C.
Berndt 1945, 1964; R. Berndt 1970:216-247; Gould 1969a; Mountford
1937-9; Mountford and Tonkinson 1969:371-390; Tindale 1936.

[5] The Aborigines say that the carved wooden boards carried by the ancestral
beings all metamorphosed into stone. Aboriginal men also carve wooden
boards. Small ones, such as bull-roarers and those used in love magic, are
kept in small bags together with other sacred objects belonging to initiated
men, but all the large boards, which are owned by the collectivity, are kept
in storehouses at a special ground in "men's country" near the settlement.
While Aborigines freely acknowledge that these boards are not *maɲundjanu*
'from the Dreamtime,' they are nevertheless sacred and are considered extremely dangerous to all but initiated men.

The many hundreds of myths known to the Jigalong people can be divided into two types: the more common and apparently more important type is the descriptive narrative, which relates the travels of ancestral beings and is replete with place names and with brief accounts of the ancestral beings' creation of natural features and of their meetings with other beings. These myths tend to be lengthy and center on major ancestral beings whose exploits are also encapsulated in songlines associated with important rituals. Such myths flesh out the skeleton provided by the songs, which are very short and at best are cryptic and make oblique references to certain Dreamtime events. An excerpt follows from the Two Men myth, an extremely long narrative of the travels of these creative beings in the Western Desert and beyond.

> The Two Men traveled on until they reached a spot where they put down all their gear and camped. They named it Djilbiṛiri. Then they went on to a place where they pierced each other's nasal septum; they named it Mulajidibuṛa, a big rock with a hole through it. They went on, and saw a small kangaroo lying down; they backtracked, then crept up on it and speared it. They cooked and ate the meat and called the place Wirgudja. Back again they went. They broke down some spear-trees, put the shafts over a fire, straightened, then sharpened them. "Good spearwood?" asked the Milaŋga man. "We will make barbs," he said, and they did. They carved signature patterns onto their spears, rubbed fat on them, sang some of their own songline, the Walawalaṇu, called the place Woguḷaṛa, then went on to Wangaḍaŋga and camped there.

The other main type of myth is best described as a situational one, in which the site of the myth is either not given or is not important to the events depicted, because the emphasis is on situation and character interaction. This kind of myth often validates a particular practice or a characteristic of some variety of fauna, as in the following example:

> Galaja Gaṛimara and Ɖanudi Banaga, the emu and the bustard (scrub turkey), were two *wadjira* (cross-cousin "sisters") who were camping together. One day, Emu, the younger "Z," went off into the bush with her big mob of emu chicks. There, she hid all but two of them. When she returned to camp, Bustard asked her where the rest of her children were. Emu lied, saying that she had killed off all but two of them. Bustard was then so ashamed of all her children and so sorry for her "Z" Emu that she immediately killed all but two of her

own children. Whereupon Emu left the camp, gathered her hidden
children from the bush, then returned with them, laughing at the
joke she had played. Bustard was very angry and decided to get
revenge at some future time. One day Bustard took her remaining
children with her and camped out in the bush, where she hunted
grasshoppers. Then she returned to camp with a chick under each
wing, and with her wings hanging limply as if both were broken.
She wailed to Emu, "Poor me! I broke my wings because I was so
sorry from thinking about my dead children!" Emu then became
very ashamed and sorry for her "Z," so she cut her own wings in
sympathy. Whereupon Bustard flew triumphantly into the air and
cried out, "Look at me, look at me you lot! I've taken off and I'm
flying!" and she sang out her call as she swooped by. Too late,
Emu realized that she too had been tricked. From that day hence,
emus have not been able to fly, and bustards lay only one or two
eggs.

Many situational myths are known to women and children,
whereas much of the longer narrative myths is known only to
initiated men. These two myth types are never mutually exclusive, however; narratives often mention practices that validate,
or are cited to validate, the Law, and they sometimes dwell on
character interaction, but generally at a given site.

Totemism

Aboriginal Australian totemism has long been a contentious
topic in anthropological circles, yet its significance in Aboriginal
society is still not particularly clear.[6] Space does not permit me
to enter the debate here, so the following discussion is restricted
to the phenomenon as it exists at Jigalong.

Western Desert Aborigines share what can be termed a to-
temistic world view. They conceptualize a single, unified cosmic
order in which man and the natural species, ancestral beings,
spirits, and other conceived entities are on equal terms. All are
interrelated in a genealogical and pseudo-genealogical manner,
and some form of communication is possible among all of them.

---

[6] Some of the writers who deal with Australian Aboriginal totemism in
some detail are: R. and C. Berndt 1964:189-198; Elkin 1954:132-155;
Lévi-Strauss 1963; Radcliffe-Brown 1952:117-132; Strehlow 1970:92-140;
Worsley 1967:141-159.

Whatever animal form ancestral beings may have assumed, they are thought of by Aborigines as being also human in form and behavior, sometimes both human and animal simultaneously; but only if this distinction becomes crucial to the plot is the human-animal division made by the narrator.

Jigalong Aborigines know the section membership of all the ancestral beings and frequently refer to them by kinship terms. Aboriginal man does not talk to the trees, but, depending on his particular totemic connection and territorial affiliation, he believes he can communicate with spirits who are responsible for the continued growth and fertility of flora and fauna which emanate from specific sites, known as *djabija,* 'increase centers.'[7] He is bound to his totemic ancestors and spirits by putative genealogy and can therefore expect reciprocity from them for his ritual services, just as he expects it from the kinsmen to whom he is linked by ties of obligation and responsibility.

Several different kinds of totemism are discernible at Jigalong, but for the purposes of this study, it is appropriate to focus on the two major kinds: conception and ancestral totemism.

Conception Totemism. Every Jigalong Aborigine has a *njuga* (or *djarinba*) 'conception totem,' and a few people possess two. The totem may be a plant, animal, insect, secretion, or mineral, the name of which is frequently given to the person, with the result that his or her totem is known to all other local people. A person does not generally feel any special affection for or emotional bond with his conception totem. He adopts no special ritual attitude towards it, and he may eat it.[8]

The conception totem is a manifestation of *djidjigargal* 'spirit-children' who are said to have inhabited certain hilly areas and large trees since the Dreamtime and travel far afield at times

---

[7] Although the term "increase center" is in common anthropological use, it is not strictly accurate. As Meggitt notes, with regard to "increase" ceremonies, "The participants are simply concerned to maintain the supplies of natural species at their usual level, to support the normal order of nature." (1962:221)

[8] This is not the case in many other parts of Aboriginal Australia, where totemites are said to have felt a strong emotional bond with their totem, as same "flesh," and therefore refrained from harming or eating it.

in search of their mothers. The totem is usually identified when a woman feels ill or vomits after eating a certain food. Some peculiarity in the appearance or taste of the food, or its over-abundance at a particular spot, suggests to the woman or her husband that it was actually a spirit-child, which has assumed the form of this particular food and has found and entered its mother. Later, when the child is born, its relatives look for fur-ther signs — birthmarks or blemishes — that will verify its con-ception totem; thus many people identify digging stick or spear marks on their bodies and believe that these were inflicted by their mother or father while they were still in plant or animal form as spirit-children.

Despite variation in individual conceptions of the spirit-child and its activities, it is clear that traditionally the spiritual dimension of parenthood was strongly emphasized, at the ex-pense of whatever knowledge the Aborigines may have possessed of physiological aspects of paternity and maternity. This re-mains true today, regardless of information to the contrary that many Aborigines have gleaned from whites.[9]

Ancestral Totemism. This term is analogous to "cult totem-ism" (Elkin 1954:143-152), but the term "cult" is inappropriate in the Jigalong situation. During their extensive travels, the an-cestral beings left objects behind, such as weapons, body exuviae, and down-feathers from their body decorations, which were ani-mated with a kind of life-force or power. From this life-essence came spirit-children who waited in plant or animal form until they could be born as Aborigines. Ancestral and conception totemism are thus interrelated, in that both owe their existence to the life-force that was part of all ancestral beings and all their possessions.

Any child conceived or born in the vicinity of the route of a particular ancestral being or group of beings is identified with them as his ancestral totem. At Jigalong, the way to ask for

---

[9] During the past few decades there has been a protracted and interesting de-bate among anthropologists as to whether or not Australian Aborigines are aware of the part played by semen in physiological paternity, and the question remains an open one in the sense that both sides have presented con-vincing evidence to support their views. See, for example, Ashley-Montagu 1937, 1940; R. and C. Berndt 1945:77-83. 1964:121-123; Elkin 1954:165; Kaberry 1939:43; Warner 1937/64:24.

someone's ancestral totem is, *ŋanalunda ganu djunu janu*? 'Who carried you, left you and went on?' Although most adults were born in the estates of their fathers, their ancestral totem need not coincide with that of their father, because any given area may have several ancestral tracks crossing it.

Despite these shared ancestral totems, people so connected do not necessarily feel a special bond with one another and are in no way committed to act on this basis; that is, there are no totemic cults as such, and there is no evidence to suggest that such groups operated in precontact times. Social totemism (a close bond between a social group and a given totem) is not important in the culture of the Aborigines at Jigalong, despite the fact that it appears to have been widespread in Aboriginal Australia. During rituals that concern major ancestral beings, the allocation of roles to singers and dancers is not based on totemic affiliations. Likewise, the possession of a particular totem does not usually give the person concerned any special privilege or responsibility during the performance of a ritual that includes his totem (with the exception of increase rites, discussed below). The major rituals and songlines, which have diffused widely throughout the Western Desert, have long ceased to be the property of any one group and are instead held in common and performed by responsible elders and initiated men, regardless of ancestral or other kinds of totemic affiliation.

The annual performance of ceremonies at increase sites, designed to "bring up" the particular plant or animal species concerned, was apparently the responsibility of initiated members of the local group, who were united by their guardianship of sites in their estate, whether or not they possessed the species concerned as their particular ancestral totem. [10] This fact, plus the great importance of transmission of religious lore in the traditional desert culture, help to explain the lack of cult totemism in the area.

Jigalong Aborigines appear to be less interested in their ancestral totem than in their conception totem, and in fact many young people are uncertain as to their ancestral totem. They do

---

[10] Descriptions of increase rites are given by R. and C. Berndt 1945:149-153, 1964:227-231; Spencer and Gillen 1938:167-211.

not generally converse much about either kind of totem. Any observer who attempted to use the concept of totemism as a heuristic tool for the explanation of cult activities, role allocation, or group affiliation would make very little headway. I agree with Stanner that the "totemic idiom" is not in itself interesting religiously, because it is a somewhat obvious means of symbolizing significant Dreamtime events by familiar things in the natural environment. What is of great importance, though, is the way in which totemism reflects the Aborigines' oneness with the natural world and with the other conceived inhabitants of their cosmic order.

Magic

As in all Aboriginal societies, Jigalong has a number of men (approximately fifteen) who are said to possess a *maban*, a magical object or objects kept within their bodies — usually in the stomach — and which has both curative and destructive powers. These men are the native doctors, who are also called *maban* and function as part-time specialists. Many have spirit-familiars which aid them in their frequent and allegedly efficient communication with the spiritual world. Most native doctors inherit their special powers from their fathers, and are said to be able to see inside people in order to diagnose and treat illness. They are also presumed to be capable of harming others, but this aspect of their capacities is not socially sanctioned, so its existence is denied by the doctors. [11]

Aborigines frequently call upon native doctors to treat illness magically, to divine the causes of epidemics, to find lost objects, and to protect people against attacks by malignant spirits. The doctors are also said to act as leaders on dream-spirit journeys which Aborigines often take during dreams. Most journeys are said to be undertaken in large groups as a safety precaution, because such trips into the desert often include visits to sacred sites. There, the travelers may encounter spirit children,

---

[11] Many writers have commented on the role of native doctors in Aboriginal society, but the most comprehensive account is provided by Elkin 1945.

malevolent spirits, and other beings that could cause illness
if the native doctors were not present to ward off the evils. The
reality of such journeys is unquestioned by the Aborigines. One
morning I met a young man who looked utterly exhausted, so I
asked him what was wrong; he replied, "Christ, I feel proper bug-
gared (tired out) today — went *baḍundjari* ('dream-spirit') last
night right up to the Kimberlies!" (an area several hundred miles
north of Jigalong). The important part played by dream-spirit
journeys in the religious life of the local people is discussed later.[12]

Because the only deaths that Aborigines attribute to natural
causes are those of the very old and the very young, the practice
of sorcery is believed by Jigalong people to be widespread and
common to all Aboriginal groups. Open accusations are sometimes
exchanged by community members after a sudden death has occurred.
At such times, the distrust between the two main linguistic
groups surfaces in private conversations, when people voice their
suspicions about who is responsible for the tragedy. Traditionally,
inquests were held, usually when the deceased's bones were ex-
humed and prepared for final burial, and a particular individual or
group was marked for revenge, but this practice has lapsed in the
contact situation.

Because sorcery accusations and counter-accusations occur
both within and between Aboriginal communities, they have considerable disruptive potential. Thus, at the time of the "big meetings" each year, participating groups must attempt to settle all outstanding disputes so that subsequent ritual activities are not inter-
rupted or marred by conflict. The Law demands peace at such
times, and men must participate with "good feelings" in their sto-
machs to ensure that the meetings will be a success.

Many deaths are attributed to the malicious and deadly activities of featherfeet ritual killers (*djinagarbil*, 'bound feet,' refers
to the special moccasins worn by these men to disguise their
tracks). Featherfeet are said to be men, not spirits, who come
from distant areas and lie in wait for their victims, whom they
ambush, kill, revive magically, then send back to Camp. The victim is said to remember nothing of the attack and has no visible

---

[12] For a fuller account of the role of the dream-spirit at Jigalong, see
Tonkinson 1970:277-291.

wounds, yet dies within days and is unable to name his attackers. Many night rituals at Jigalong are brought to a sudden and dramatic halt after someone claims to have seen or heard featherfeet in the vicinity. Children sometimes terrify one another with vivid stories of alleged featherfeet atrocities. Some of the older men at the mission claim to have participated in *wanmala* 'revenge expeditions' as featherfeet in desert times. These men have the little toe on each foot dislocated upwards. This was done during ritual preparations to allow the toes to act as eyes in the dark and prevent the men from treading on dry sticks which would reveal their presence to the victim. Several pairs of featherfeet moccasins are in the possession of older men, but significantly, no one claims to have ever killed anybody during such expeditions. [13]

Ritual

Although ritual activity reaches its peak of intensity during the midsummer "big meetings," it is never far from the minds of Jigalong men, and there is always some kind of ritual business being planned, discussed, or enacted at the mission, regardless of season. Ritual is the most important concern of the adults, who see it as essential to their well-being because of its underlying positive sanctions — continued harmonious relations between man, nature, and the spiritual realm — and also because of their belief that the cessation of ritual will result in the withdrawal of reciprocity by the spiritual beings. It is through ritual in particular that Aboriginal adults act for the entire community in following faithfully and confidently the life-design that is their unique heritage from the Dreamtime, a source of power that non-Aborigines can neither comprehend nor usurp.

Power. The ordering and control of power is a recurrent theme in all religions (cf. Burridge 1969:5). It is basic to the Aboriginal world view, in which all power is derived from the Dreamtime and is concentrated in the spiritual beings. Because the

---

[13] This set of beliefs concerning the existence and activities of featherfeet killers is widespread in the desert areas and has been reported on by many anthropologists; see, for example, R. and C. Berndt 1945:177-180, 1964: 271-273; Spencer and Gillen 1938:476-496.

Dreamtime is simultaneously of the past and present, the powers immanent in the many sites where Dreamtime events occurred are still available for Aboriginal man (Stanner 1966:164). Through the performance of ritual, the undertaking of dream-spirit journeys, acts of revelation by spirit intermediaries, the touching and contemplation of highly sacred objects, and other religious acts, man can enter the spiritual realm and tap this reservoir of power.

The performance of ritual is not just the principal method of communicating with spirits in order to activate reciprocal obligations; it is also the means by which individuals can enter the spiritual realm and come into direct contact with the great powers of the Dreamtime. As preexisting spirit-children, Aborigines were once part of that realm, and as spirits after death they will ultimately return there; but they also must have access to it during their lifetime as human beings if they are to maintain their strength and self-identity. A dancer is not merely imitating the activities of a particular ancestral being; for the duration of his dance he transcends himself and *becomes* that being, entering into the spiritual realm and remaining there until, at the end of his performance, he is tapped on the shoulder to bring him back into the physical world. Whatever the ritual, Aborigines attempt to become one with the Dreamtime, to draw power from it, and to comprehend more fully their place in the cosmic order. From such emotionally charged experiences they learn, and through their increased knowledge, they change.

The Concept of the Sacred. This concept is strongly developed in most Aboriginal societies and is usually conveyed by words that translate as 'set apart,' 'forbidden,' 'dangerous,' 'from the Dreamtime' (R. and C. Berndt 1964:186-188). Sacred objects and activities generally pertain to the Dreamtime and are repositories of life-essence or power. The danger inherent in things classified as sacred is mainly related to novices coming into contact with sacred elements for the first time, and to the uninitiated. Although the great majority of secret-sacred rituals and related activities are restricted to initiated men, there are certain rituals held by adult women which are secret-sacred to themselves, and all males and children are excluded. The necessity of shielding the uninitiated from the dangers of the sacred results in the designation of certain areas surrounding the mission as "men's country," forbidden to all others. Here the men store sacred objects

Plate 7. Division into generation level groupings during ritual: men of the two groupings circle senior women upon arrival in Camp from the secret bush ground.

and build ceremonial grounds for the performance of secret-sacred rituals. Even the smallest children know the directions they must never go when they wander from the Camp.

Ritual Divisions. Previous mention was made of generation level groups that characterize many Jigalong rituals and are discernible in seating arrangements and the expression of ritual opposition. The Aborigines' choice of this form of dual organization may have been prompted by the fact that it effectively separates a person from his or her *umaṛi*; i.e. "sons-in-law" from "mothers-in-law," who must strictly avoid each other. By physically separating members of adjacent generation levels, between most of whom some form of restraint behavior is the norm, this kind of division obviates the need for constant concern with avoidance behavior during ritual activity, particularly at night when it is often difficult to identify individuals in a crowd.

Also, those who are opposed ritually and can thus openly but jokingly chastise one another are mainly those who sometimes have conflicting interests in everyday life, for example as wife-givers and wife-receivers, and as the women involved in such transactions. The alternating generation level division could thus be viewed as a relatively harmless way of channeling potential conflict or aggression into a socially sanctioned ritual context. The kind of ritual opposition expressed at such times is never destructive or truly divisive. In general, a spirit of cooperation between members of the two groups is always present.

Ritual Statuses. An Aborigine's status is largely a concomitant of sex and age, and Aboriginal society is principally concerned with kinship status. The only non-kinbased statuses that are named and ranked are those associated with an individual's progression through the life cycle, and a few that exist in the religious life. A major division exists between those men who are subincised and those who are not, and the male initiation process contains a number of named intermediate stages through which a novice must pass before being considered fully initiated and therefore eligible to marry.

Among fully initiated men, there is a broad division into older men who have attained the position of cooks for the periodic *midajidi* 'ritual feasts,' and those middle-aged and younger men who are the hunters. The latter must supply fresh meat to be eaten with the large breadcakes (called dampers) cooked by the ritual feast elders. The meat is a general payment rendered to those who are instructing their juniors in ritual aspects of the Law, but all initiated men partake of both damper and meat during such feasts. Ritual feast elders periodically elect new men, who have been conscientious upholders of the Law for a long time, to the rank of cook. Several elders are also charged with the custodianship of the storehouses that contain the carved wooden boards. The custodians clean and prepare the storehouse area for ritual activities, and they must keep the sacred boards well oiled and clean.

As previously mentioned, every ritual known to the Jigalong people involves certain elders who are acknowledged as its "head bosses" and are charged with the organization and direction of the performances. There is no special term for this status, and the incumbents vary according to which ritual is being staged. The men who were initiated earliest, have participated most often in the ritual, and know best its contents are the headmen, in most cases, regardless of totemic affiliation.

There is also a broad division of the adult women into ritual feast cooks and others. Because the burden of maintaining the religious life and the community's spiritual well-being lies princi-

pally in the hands of the men, the role of women in this aspect of
the culture is generally a peripheral one. Female cooks are chosen
from the old and middle-aged by the male ritual feast cooks, and
they do the actual mixing and kneading of the dampers while the
men tend the fires and cook. Older women are also the "head
bosses" for the few secret-sacred rituals that they perform, most
often during "big meetings," to the exclusion of males and the
uninitiated.

Ritual Types. For purposes of clarification, the many different rituals that are performed at Jigalong may be conveniently
divided into three main categories according to who is involved,
the alleged origin of the ritual, and its apparent overall purpose.

Personnel Involved. The term secret-sacred refers to rituals
held out of sight of Camp which involve fully initiated members
of the same sex with the exclusion of opposite sex members and
the uninitiated. Such rituals, however, may include some novices
who are witnessing them for the first time. Most of the dances
and associated paraphernalia are considered sacred and thus very
dangerous to all but the fully initiated.

A second kind of ritual involves some initiated members of
both sexes at the same time, and perhaps at the same place, to the
exclusion of all uninitiated persons. For instance, in some cases
most men are away in the bush performing secret-sacred rituals,
while near the Camp a group composed of male and female ritual
feast cooks prepares dampers to be eaten by the men when they
return.

In the third ritual type, men, women, and children assemble
at once, generally in or close to the main Camp area. The women
can sing and dance in some of these rituals, and the children may
also participate; they are thus popular because virtually the entire
community is involved. The presence of both sexes and children
indicates that secret-sacred objects or dances are absent. However,
many such rituals conclude with special dances during which secret-sacred objects are displayed, and at such times all women and
children are instructed to keep their heads hidden under blankets
until the objects have been removed, and it is again safe for them
to witness the proceedings.

Origin. The Aborigines make a distinction between rituals
which are allegedly *manundjanu* 'from the creative period' and
those which are known to be *badundjaridjanu* 'from the dream-

spirit.' The great majority of rituals performed at Jigalong are said to have been composed during the Dreamtime by ancestral beings and to have been handed on by countless generations of Aborigines to the present. Less common, but nonetheless important in the local religious life, are those of the second type, rituals composed by local men after they had been 'given' by spirit-beings during travels the men undertake, or believe they undertake, during dreams. One of these rituals is usually composed every few years and is sung and performed periodically until replaced by a newly composed successor. Meanwhile, the older one has usually been handed on to groups from other Law centers and begins its journey around the desert periphery through the normal channels of intercommunity cultural transmission.

One dream-spirit ritual of local origin was composed in 1962 by ten men of mixed linguistic group affiliations. It consists of about 120 verses and has as its central theme weather phenomena— rain, clouds, lightning, and thunder — and associated beings. It is called Winba or Djaramara, from the names of the major rainmaking ancestor.[14]

Such rituals originated in informal discussions among initiated men, many of them native doctors, who have songs, dances, and associated sacred objects revealed to them by spirit-beings they encounter in dream-spirit journeys. When several men report similar experiences, they can then establish a theme. As more men dream and "find" songs and dances these are added to the line, which is later learned by members of both sexes. Each such ritual has a distinctive tune, and characteristic dance steps, body decorations, and sacred objects, but the overall form and procedures of the dream-spirit rituals are similar.

Such rituals are relatively short-lived with respect to their actual span of performances at any one settlement, and almost all their songs can be sung by members of both sexes. This is not to say that the Aborigines consider them any less valid than the rituals from the creative period. In fact, the most obvious explanation for the origin of the Dreamtime rituals is that they were pro-

---

14 For a fuller description of this dream-spirit ritual, see Mountford and Tonkinson 1969:371-390.

bably composed long ago by groups of Aborigines in much the same way as dream-spirit rituals. Over time, and with cultural transmission, the composers were quickly forgotten and Aborigines of later generations came to regard them as being Dreamtime creations. In one sense all rituals are from the Dreamtime, and they reflect the aptness of the Aborigines' choice of the English word "dreaming" to refer to the creative period, since it is mainly during dreams that contact with the spiritual realm is made and new knowledge is gained by revelation.

The number and variety of rituals 'from the Dreamtime' that are performed by the Aborigines of Jigalong is such that an adequate description of them is beyond the scope of this study. During the three month period over Christmas 1969-70, for instance, there were more than seventy performances of at least thirteen different rituals, several of which had been recently introduced from the south. Later in this chapter, brief mention will be made of some of the major rituals.

Purpose. The classification of rituals according to their purpose or intent is no easy task, since any given situation can be interpreted as fulfilling several different but complementary functions in Aboriginal society. For example, it could be safely said that at Jigalong, a nontraditional community comprised of several different linguistic groups from widely separated home areas, the shared religious life transcends the former divisions that have potential for conflict, and the cooperation involved in the creation of dream-spirit rituals and the performance of all rituals reinforces the growing ethnocentrism and in-group solidarity of the Jigalong mob. Thus all rituals are integratory elements in promoting Aboriginal ethnocentrism and a sense of security among those who subscribe to the society's basic values embodied in the concept of the Law. Nevertheless, it is useful to group rituals according to their principal underlying purpose, and this produces the following divisions:

Initiation. Two major rituals are specifically associated with the early part of the male initiation process, which at Jigalong begins with circumcision, then proceeds through subincision and several other stages which, ideally, should precede marriage. One of these rituals is the Njungunj (or Milgu), which is "from the creative period" and is secret-sacred to initiated men in its entirety. This ritual, which is performed at a ground far from the Camp,

Plate 8. Heavily anointed with blood, a post-circumcision novice is observed by uninitiated boys following his ceremonial reentry into Camp at the end of his seclusion period.

centers mainly on the exploits of Maḷu, the ancestral kangaroo-man, who appears to be the best known Western Desert ancestral being. It consists of hundreds of short verses and a great many dances, and is sung before, during, and after both circumcision and subincision, mainly during daylight hours. The associated dances are performed late in the afternoon following several hours of spirited singing, as the assembled men trace in song the route of Maḷu and many associated ancestral beings. During "big meetings" this ritual is often held at the same time as certain other rituals which can be performed in Camp at night, so that women and children can attend the latter and do not feel left out of the action.

The other ritual closely associated with initiation, but held much less often, is the Walawalaṇu or Djindjun, which concerns the travels and adventures of Wadi Gudjara, the Two Men. This ritual, also secret-sacred to initiated men, begins in the camp of the novice after circumcision when his penis is almost healed, and also at the storehouse of sacred boards during the *midajidi* (another initiatory ritual) when the sacred boards are first revealed to a group of novices. The main Walawalanu performance is an all-night affair to mark the boy's "rebirth" into adulthood and his return to the Camp. In contrast to the Njungunj, few dances are associated with this ritual, but on the final night, older men point out to the novice, during the singing of relevant songs, all the important ancestral beings that are visible in star or galaxy form. At dawn, the boy is anointed with blood drawn from the arms of the assembled men, and then is chased noisily back into Camp where the women tearfully welcome him, and the smaller children stand around to verify that he has survived the ordeal. With his thick coat of blood, however, he looks much the worse for wear.

Ancestral-Instructive. Most of the rituals performed at Jigalong belong to this category, in that they concern the acting out of what Stanner aptly calls the "founding dramas" or "marvels" of the Dreamtime, embodied in a corpus of myths, songs, and dances (1965:213-214). As with the two initiation rituals just mentioned, these performances have an instructive aspect, because there are almost always some novices present, and some explanations, however cryptic, are offered by elders who know the ritual well. Formal instruction as such is minimal in most cases, because the emphasis is on the naming and identification of objects and associated ancestral beings. The elders impress upon the novices the secret-sacred and dangerous character of the names and information they divulge during the course of the ritual. Through repeated attendance at the same ritual, younger men gain a clearer understanding of its mythological background.

Commemorative-Recreational. Included in this category are the dream-spirit rituals, which can be regarded as the acting out and commemorating of the verses, dances, and objects revealed to Aborigines during their dream-spirit journeys. Because women and children can witness most of the activity, these rituals function as recreational forms in a more general way than do most of the other kinds of ritual, which mainly concern smaller segments of the settlement population. Nevertheless, the great enjoyment that Aborigines derive from all their ritual activities is immediately obvious to an outsider.

Increase. The physical separation of the Jigalong Aborigines from their original home territories and increase centers precludes the performance of the small seasonal rites traditionally held at

such sites. The ceremonies were usually simple, and were performed by several male local group elders. They visited the site,
cleaned around it, perhaps polished and anointed the stones with
blood from their arms, then talked to the spirits of the particular
species believed to be living within and asked them to emerge and
be plentiful across the land.

One very interesting post-migration development at the mission is the use by local Aborigines of dream-spirit journeys to return periodically to their estates in the desert where they visit the
increase centers to "bring up" the species for which they are responsible. That is, the Aborigines, or certain elders and native
doctors among them, believe that they do revisit the increase sites
and can still ensure the continuation of the associated species without actually having to trek across the desert to the sites. They say
that they had the power of flight long before whites developed
it, and that such journeys, though fraught with dangers at times,
are relatively effortless. It appears, then, that dream-spirit journeys have come to assume increased significance as the only ave-
nue of contact utilized by the Aborigines between the settlement
and their desert homelands. This is the means by which the Aborigines can continue to maintain vital, life-sustaining ties with
the desert proper.

In a very general sense it could be argued that all rituals have,
for the Aborigines, an increase function, because man and the natural species can be assured of continued existence and fertility
only through the continued performance of ritual. The performance of some major rituals is said to promote the increase of the
animals and birds whose exploits are depicted in their songlines
and dances. For example, the Njungunj is thought to "bring up"
kangaroos as well as the other natural species featured in this
ritual.

One very important ritual performed every summer at Jigalong can be classed as an increase rite despite the fact that in its
scale and organizational complexity it is a larger and more drawn
out ritual than any other at the settlement. This is the Ŋa:wajil, a
ritual imported from the north in the early 1960s but already
known to many older Jigalong men who had been initiated into it
in desert times. The Ŋa:wajil is of central concern to the Aborigines because it is a rainmaking ritual, and rain is a scarce commod-
ity in the desert. It concerns Winba, an old snake-man ancestral

being, and his fellow Djaṛamara rainmaking beings, who control all rain, clouds, thunder, lightning, hail, and related weather phenomena. From a survey of the literature on Australian Aboriginal rainmaking practices, I concluded that the ŋa:wajil is the longest and most complex of all rainmaking rituals reported on. It is the only one that is characterized by a clearly defined status hierarchy, a duration of many days, a number of simultaneous ceremonial activities enacted each day, and events that involve the entire community at certain times. [15]

Only a brief outline of the general format and activities involved in the ŋa:wajil need be given here. No other Jigalong ritual approaches the complexity of the ŋa:wajil, which is atypical in its elaborate status hierarchy, consisting of five male and four female grades, all named and differentiated according to insignia, ritual responsibility, and functions. This elaboration of statuses probably stems from the ritual's complexity, which necessitates an efficient division of labor for the coordination and enactment of several different activities in different locations at the same time. According to the Aborigines, they must perform the ŋa:wajil every year in order to "bring up" rain and also to initiate novices into the ritual. Following their initiation, men must participate repeatedly in subsequent performances of the ritual so that they can be elevated in the status hierarchy.

ŋa:wajil activities center on two main ceremonial grounds. At the *njinjinganu,* close to Camp, the entire community assembles each day at certain times, men and women of appropriate status prepare and cook dampers, the men eat *wanaburga* 'ŋa:wajil feasts' when they return from the bush, and much singing, dancing, and water throwing take place. The other ground, the *baljbara,* hidden in "men's country" away from Camp, is where the secret-sacred rainmaking objects are set up, singing and dancing take place, and initiates are introduced to the vitally important and secret aspects of encouraging rainmaking ancestors to send rain. The objects, two conical piles of lightning, thunder, hail, and rainbow stones, lengths of hairstring, pearlshells, and other objects, are anointed with arm-blood ("rain"), covered with down feathers

---

[15] A survey of rainmaking practices in Aboriginal Australia and a detailed description of the ŋa:wajil ritual are given in Tonkinson 1972:64-197.

from eaglehawks ("clouds"), "fed" with pieces of damper and water, and danced around and contemplated by the initiated men present. The rainmaking snakes believed to live in the piles are said to communicate directly with the original rainmaking increase sites and will respond favorably to correct ritual activities. Visits to the increase sites by large numbers of Aborigines in dream-spirit form are considered to be an essential part of the ŋa:wajil and must be undertaken if the rain is to find its way back to the Jigalong area.

Throughout the ritual, and particularly during the activities that take place at and around the Camp ceremonial ground, there is a clear division between the two generation level groupings. Each group works separately in the purchase, storage, preparation, supervision, and consumption of its own food supplies, although these activities take place concurrently during the ritual. At the Camp ground, the two groups (including men and women of each) sit at opposite ends of a long boughshed constructed specially for the ritual, and most dancing in the Camp area is done in two groups according to this division. An exciting feature of the ritual is the frequent expression of opposition between members of the two groups, which takes the form of lighthearted abuse and spectacular water-throwing battles, in which the aim is to douse certain kin in the opposite group. Although in the Camp sections of the ritual women and children neither sing nor dance much, the women participate actively in the water-throwing, and everyone enjoys these prolonged bouts. Since the temperature is generally well over 100° F. at such times, this showering is a refreshing experience, except when dirt is deliberately added to the water.

The many varied activities associated with the ritual are usually spread over two or three weeks, and since it involves the entire Aboriginal community at times, the ŋa:wajil is a popular event at Jigalong, especially when large groups from neighboring Law centers also participate.

Ritual Paraphernalia. The Aborigines make an important distinction between objects that can be seen by members of the opposite sex and the uninitiated, and those that can be seen only by initiated members of the same sex, and perhaps also by novices undergoing initiation into particular rituals. Paraphernalia belonging to the first category include the woolen and hairstring bands worn by men on their foreheads, necks, and upper arms, white

Plate 9. Rainmaking ritual: women of one generation level grouping wait to throw water over men of the opposing group as the latter dance onto the Camp ground upon their return from the bush.

forehead bands, pearlshell necklets (worn by some members of both sexes), upper arm ornaments and pubic pendants (worn only by men and usually made of engraved pearlshell), bundles of wood shavings worn in armbands and across the forehead by men, and bunches of green leaves held in the hands and shaken during dances by both sexes. Fat, red ochre, and blood are used by the men on their bodies, usually in association with various body designs. Women do not use blood on their bodies. Most body decorations can be seen by members of the opposite sex and the uninitiated, but certain patterns are secret-sacred and must be rubbed off carefully before the people return to Camp.

The women have some secret-sacred objects but I know nothing of these in any detail. The men, of course, have many. In some rituals they wear elaborate headdresses, facepieces, or tails, constructed from grass wrapped in old rags and used only in the bush. Lengths of twine, covered with red ochre and fat, are the principal decoration in certain of the more recently introduced southern rituals. A great variety of objects worn or carried during dances are lumped together under the generic term *wanigi.* All such objects are variants on the thread-cross; they can be used only

once, and must then be dismantled and rethreaded for later use. [16]
These thread-crosses range in size from the little kangaroo 'ears,'
raba, to fencelike constructions over thirty feet long made by join-
ing sacred boards and spears together to form a framework on
which wool and hairstring are threaded. Although a large *wanigi*
may take a team of men half a day or more to construct, they are
used in dances that rarely last more than four or five minutes.

Secret-sacred carved wooden boards form a category of their
own. These boards, ranging in size from a few inches to nearly
twenty feet, are man-made replicas of the boards that all ancestral
beings are said to have carried with them and deposited at all important sites throughout the desert. The cutting and carving of a
sacred board is the most important final step in the initiation process for males. Typically, the carved pattern on a board is a styl-
ized representation of a stretch of country or site and an associated ancestral being or beings generally, but not necessarily, linked
totemically to the carver. Men are expected to continue cutting
and carving boards throughout their lives until their hands become
too unsteady to manage the fine chisel work. Most boards are
considered the property of the collectivity regardless of the carver,
but some of the smaller boards, particularly those of the bull-
roarer type, are owned individually and are kept in saddlebags or
other containers close to Camp. All boards have potential utility
for sorcery, wherein a board is "loaded" with power, then pointed
and "fired" in the general direction of the victim who later sickens
and dies. They are regarded as extremely dangerous to the uninitiated and are kept well hidden at all times. Traditionally, it is said
that any woman or uninitiated person who inadvertently saw these
boards would turn blind or would be killed.

The most important objects in the religious life are secret-
sacred polished stones that can be seen only by middle-aged and
older men. These stones are regarded as the most sacred objects
because of their supposedly direct link with the ancestral beings,

---

16 This object consists of two crossed wooden sticks, threaded with hairstring or woolen yarn, into a diamond shape. It is similar in form to the
thread-crosses of the Huichol Indians (of the Mexican states of Nayarit and
Jalisco), which are widely imitated and sold to tourists in Mexico.

who either left them behind or else metamorphosed into them.
A few are carved, like the well-known Aranda *tjurunga* (cf. Strehlow 1947:84) and many are shaped and polished, but such modifications are firmly believed to be the work of Dreamtime beings.
Most have unusual colors and textures, which lend credence to
their alleged Dreamtime origin, and although most of them have
no particular ritual usage — other than being touched, rubbed, and
contemplated — they are believed to be major repositories of life-
force or power.

   The location of the sacred stones is usually revealed to Aboriginal men by spirit-children during dreams or in waking life.
Their shape, as well as the Aborigines' knowledge of ancestral
paths through particular areas, lead to their identification. If there
is some doubt, native doctors at the settlement are consulted, and
with the local elders, they identify the ancestral associations of the
stones. Many of these stones eventually enter the intercommunity
transmission circuit and are handed on, amid great precautions,
from neighboring Law centers, for further contemplation and discussion as tangible proof of the reality of the Dreamtime and its
relevance for the present. In January 1970, for instance, the Jigalong elders gave their southern visitors nine such stones, associated
with Emu, Eaglehawk, and Two Men, to take back to the Laverton
area with them. Two of the Two Men stones were shaped exactly
like a meat cleaver and a revolver. In answer to my comment on
this, one of the men remarked, "Yes, our ancestral beings had all
that gear in the Dreamtime, before the whitefellas had it." [17]

Intercommunity Contacts
and Cultural Transmission

   The religious life of the Aborigines at Jigalong cannot be considered properly without reference to the wider sociocultural bloc
of which the local community is an integral part. Traditionally,

---

[17] Because of their allegedly direct connection to the Dreamtime beings,
these objects are considered highly sacred by all Western Desert men. The
significance of this category of objects at Jigalong is very similar to the kinds
of stones reported by the Berndts at Ooldea in South Australia, which is also
within the Western Desert cultural bloc (1945:134-140).

Plate 10. Young initiated men decorate boys with lightning designs (associated with rainmaking ritual) prior to the ceremonial welcome for visiting groups arriving for Jigalong's "big meeting."

groups of Aborigines who were periodically forced out of their
home territories by prolonged dry periods were assured of hospitality in neighboring areas because of the shared religious and kinship ties with other groups in the Western Desert area. These links,
created initially by the wandering ancestral beings in the Dreamtime, were maintained through intermarriage and the annual "big
meetings" at which religious activities took precedence. In contrasting them with the Aranda of Central Australia, Strehlow notes
that "the Western Desert people borrowed religious concepts,
social norms, and artistic practices freely." (1965:131). The
cultural similarities that exist between Jigalong Aborigines and
those of other Law centers in the desert area are evidence of a
long history of cultural transmission that has continued unabated
since precontact times.

The neighboring Law centers with whose members the Jigalong people combine most often for "big meetings" are Wiluna,
Nullagine, and to a lesser extent Marble Bar-Moolyella (see Map 1),
as well as some of the remaining Njijabali people from station areas
west of the mission. Apart from the small groups of men who
sometimes take pre-circumcision novices on long tours, and a few
individual travelers, Jigalong people rarely go further south than
Wiluna or north past Moolyella, so that each Law center's sphere
of interaction is different from, but overlaps with, contiguous Law
centers. Songlines, dances, sacred objects, and other elements of
religious lore are passed on from group to group, and many eventually travel hundreds, even thousands, of miles from their point
of origin. In central Australia I have seen pearlshells and sacred
boards which originated in northwestern Australia and had traveled in a counterclockwise direction around the desert fringe and
into the interior. At Jigalong in 1963 I recorded songs almost
identical to those recorded twenty-two years earlier by R. and C.
Berndt at Ooldea, some 950 miles to the southeast. This is a good
indication of both the extent and effectiveness of interarea cultural transmission in the Western Desert.

Every year, groups of men travel to neighboring communities
to gather information about new rituals and songlines, and to
arrange venues for forthcoming "big meetings." As was the case
traditionally, messengers designated to summon Aborigines from
other centers carry hairbelts and small sacred objects — and sometimes a pre-circumcision novice — which are supposed to bind the

others to accept the invitation. During the course of the meetings, participants exchange weapons, ochre, pearlshells, sacred boards, and other objects, all of which serve to maintain links of friendship and shared religion among the groups present.

The general format of the "big meetings" is similar. The visitors, who always arrive en masse, assemble outside the settlement and decorate themselves. An air of great excitement prevails. Meanwhile, the local Aborigines who have been preparing for days, practice their dancing, and then assemble in one huge impressive group. They remain silent and hidden as the visitors enter the settlement and take their seats in a large cleared area. Amid a loud chorus of whoops and shouts, the locals suddenly swarm up from the creek bed and dance in mass formation around the visitors who then reciprocate. As soon as possible after the welcome dances, all outstanding disputes between members of the assembled communities are settled in ritual fashion in what is frequently a tense atmosphere. This must be done early so that subsequent ritual activities will take place in an atmosphere of goodwill, unmarred by conflicts.

If the visitors have been summoned to attend an initiation, which usually entails the "putting through" of several novices together, this will generally be the first order of ritual business. If, however, they have been invited to be initiated into a particular ritual, this will begin the ceremonies. There is some initiatory activity involving circumcision and subincision at every such meeting, because large numbers will be present to celebrate the novices' *rite de passage,* and because of the strong preference for men from other Law centers to perform the physical operations. A boy cannot be operated on by a close relative, and since the subsequent relationship between the pair and their close relatives is one of embarrassment and avoidance, it is preferable to choose men from other communities to operate.

With the steady increase in the number and road-worthiness of Aboriginal-owned vehicles, intercommunity communications are improving. Aborigines also make use of radio-telegraph to inform friends in other centers of their movements and to request transportation assistance. For all this, the annual gatherings rarely begin on schedule, and traveling groups invariably spend much longer on the road than intended, what with breakdowns and delays at "watering places" en route, where thirsts are not easily slaked and the beer is ice-cold. Nevertheless, it appears that news of impending meetings is spreading further now, and groups of Aborigines are moving further from their home communities than ever before to attend them. Aborigines often go to considerable trouble to make such trips. They greatly enjoy the excitement and tension of the gatherings, especially the ritual activities, which are powerful attractions and remain a major force of their tradition-orientation. During these meetings the participating Aborigines see the Law writ large; it underlines the uniqueness of their culture and bolsters their racial pride.

CHAPTER FIVE

The Acceptance of Western Cultural Elements

One inevitable result of prolonged contact between Western culture and nonliterate peoples is the transformation of the technologically weaker culture. But changes do not occur equally in all aspects of the small-scale culture and do not take place at even rates among different cultural elements that are affected by alien forms. The uneven quality of change relates very closely to the degree of acceptance that members of the recipient culture exhibit towards the Western elements. Whether or not individuals or groups accept available elements of Western culture depends on many factors, of which the most important is the prevailing value system of the recipient culture. People respond in terms of their core values, and while values themselves are susceptible to change over time, a society's value system is a powerful conservative and stabilizing force. As Foster points out, these basic values are the essence of culture, and the question of their superiority or inferiority to alien values is very difficult either to measure or to prove (1962:68). Traditional peoples generally tend to retain their basic premises regarding the origin and nature of man and his place in the cosmic order, and such beliefs resist change, despite extensive modifications in technology and other aspects of their culture.

In many acculturation studies it has been noted that items of technology are accepted more readily by non-Western peoples than are other aspects of Western culture. From the foregoing discussion, it can thus be inferred that Western material goods are not perceived by members of the recipient culture as threatening their basic values. This is particularly true of the Aborigines, who traditionally regarded secular material items as peripheral elements of culture, valued solely for their utility. The Aborigines' semi-nomadic adaptation necessitated possession of few material goods, with each item having to be portable and capable of several different uses. Aborigines evaluated themselves and others according to actions rather than the amount or quality of one's material possessions. When the Aborigines finally settled in the contact situation, they had no reservations about adopting a range of Western goods, but their motives were still utilitarian and had little if anything to do with considerations of status.

It is a widely held principle of cultural adaptation that the acceptance of an innovation depends on the degree to which it is aligned with pre-existing orientations in the recipient culture (cf. Barnett 1953). How, then, does this account for the ready acceptance of material goods by Aborigines whose former existence was characterized by a minimum of material goods? Perhaps the best explanation is one which points to an essential continuity in Aboriginal attitudes to their natural environment. In the desert the Aborigines survived by exploiting their impoverished physical environment to the fullest, using the limited technology available to them. In the postcontact environment, they retained the principle of maximum exploitation, which was best achieved by utilizing whatever material goods they could acquire from the whites, learning, as they had always done, by observation and imitation.

Years before they came into actual contact with whites, many desert Aborigines discovered and made good use of things such as cloth, tins, iron bars, and cart springs that had been abandoned by explorers in the days before more intensive incursions took place into the Western Desert. These useful alien objects must have aroused the Aborigines' interest in the newcomers. Once they had overcome their initial fear of whites, occasioned in some areas by rumors that all white men were cannibals, the Aborigines were drawn towards the settlements by their curiosity about what the whites were doing there and what other material goods they possessed.

Today, most of the Jigalong Aborigines have been in contact with whites long enough to observe both their artifacts and their behavior as representative of Western culture. In order to survive in their new social environment, the Aborigines have been obliged to adopt at least some of the trappings of the whites and have freely chosen to adopt others. But, as will be seen in the following chapter, they have not shown interest in emulating much of the nonmaterial culture of the whites.

The Aborigines are quite pragmatic in their attitudes towards Western material culture. They see that most of it is clearly superior to local forms, and much of it has no traditional parallels. Many of the new items are readily available locally, and most Aborigines can acquire them either directly by purchase or indirectly from relatives. Experimentation with new items is generally an individual matter, so their acceptance does not raise the kinds of social complications and need for group consensus that are inevitable when the alien element involved is related to values, such as a kinship system or a marriage custom, that are not readily transferable.

Material Goods

The Aborigines have incorporated many useful Western material goods into both religious and secular areas of life. Wherever such innovations have not been perceived as contravening the dictates of the Law, they have achieved unquestioned acceptance. [1]

In the religious life, for instance, sacred wooden boards are cut and carved with steel axes and chisels, which have replaced traditional cutting and carving tools of stone, bone, and animal teeth. Initiated men keep their personal sacred objects in saddlebags or in women's handbags. [2] Wool has replaced hairstring (but not entirely) for use in body decoration and for the construction of thread-crosses. Hair oil and sheep fat have largely replaced wild

---

[1] For example, Aborigines in neighboring areas frequently prefer to use razor blades or bottle-glass slivers to perform circumcision and subincision operations, but so far this innovation has been resisted at Jigalong, where the men say that they must continue to use the *djimari* 'stone knife' in the same fashion as the ancestral beings.

[2] This is an item of Western female use which has been appropriated by Aboriginal men; as a result, few Aboriginal women use these handbags. Another, but temporary, example of this kind of male appropriation occurred among a group of desert people I visited in 1963. About a week previously the

animal fat for use in cleaning sacred objects and applying ochre and body decorations. In the organization of ritual activities, many other Western innovations play important roles; vehicles for obtaining firewood and transporting people to and from ceremonial grounds, steel drums and canvas bags for the carting and storage of vital water supplies at dry bush grounds, and vegetable foods for ritual feasts.

It was previously noted that the Jigalong people rely heavily upon non-Aboriginal foodstuffs, clothing, and a range of inexpensive and practical items of hardware. Rather than reiterate lists of these items, I will outline some noteworthy features of Aboriginal acceptance patterns. Aboriginal cooking techniques are a blend of old and new; the traditional method of cooking in or on ashes is still the most popular, but sometimes saucepans or camp-ovens are used to make stews of fresh meat and vegetables. Most people now follow the Western custom of eating three meals a day, unless food runs short, whereas traditionally the normal practice was to eat only one main meal a day.[3] Anyone who is hungry can always obtain food from relatives. Aboriginal generosity, particularly towards children, is manifest in their willingness to share food; the hoarding of food has never been a feature of their life.

Clothing is worn by everyone except small children who seem to prefer running naked. Women kept their breasts covered except when nursing their children (some of whom are still breast-fed at age four or five) and during certain rituals. The tragicomic appearance, to Western eyes, of many Jigalong adults is a result of the often inappropriate and ill-fitting secondhand clothing they receive from the missionaries: faded ball-gowns, feather hats, dark suits, football sweaters with large numbers emblazoned on the

---

group had made contact with a station owner who was traveling in the area; he gave them some men's and women's clothing. When our patrol arrived at the spot, the men in the group were wearing not only the trousers they had been given, but also the dresses. Our Aboriginal guide was quite embarrassed and quickly informed the men of their mistake; within seconds they discarded the female attire. The women saw no use for the dresses, because they covered their breasts and thus denied their small children access to milk.

[3] For good accounts of Aboriginal cooking and eating habits in the Western Desert, see Gould 1967, 1969a, 1969b:253-274.

back — anything goes on! Because most of these clothes are old to begin with and are worn constantly in dirty, dusty conditions without being washed regularly, their condition deteriorates rapidly; and the clothes that are washed regularly soon succumb to the combined effects of hard water, grit, cheap soap, and severe scrubbings. With the exception of the younger adults who are concerned with personal hygiene and appearance, the Aborigines are not at all clothes-conscious and lack pride in possession. Items of clothing, like most other things, change hands frequently, and no one is judged in terms of personal appearance.

Besides clothing, most other material goods cannot long withstand the effects of the harsh desert conditions and Aboriginal indifference to their proper care and maintenance. Even "luxury" items, such as vehicles, radios, rifles, and watches, are subject to loan or appropriation by relatives who feel that they have a right to them. Vehicle owners are constantly under pressure from their kin to run errands, get firewood or water, and take them to neighboring stations. All these requests are viewed within the matrix of kin obligations, so the question of reimbursement for such services is never raised. Besides, the "good" Aborigine is defined in terms of unselfishness and service to others, so the readiness to share one's material goods is an integral part of the assessment of individual worth in the community.

It was noted previously that there is a small hospital and outpatient clinic at the mission, run by a trained nurse who is also a missionary. Local Aborigines eagerly accept all forms of medicine, but favor injections because these are believed to be particularly powerful healing agents. These alien medicines are used by the Aborigines as supplements to traditional curative techniques. The native doctors have lost none of their clientele to the mission clinic, and they continue to perform "operations" by withdrawing "bad" blood and other foreign bodies from their patients, using a combination of pummeling, massage, biting, sucking, and sleight-of-hand.

Special mention must be made of the Aborigines' constant and strong demand for tobacco, which they chew or smoke. Most older Aborigines of both sexes chew plug tobacco by mixing it with fine powdered bark ash just as they did with wild tobaccos in precontact times. Younger people prefer to smoke cigarettes and most roll their own. Because tobacco is not stocked at the

mission store, it is usually in short supply, and anyone known to
have some is persistently pressured to share it. There are always
people wandering around in search of tobacco. Habitual beggars
may be refused, but this is rarely done directly because to do so
would contradict the Aboriginal ethos of sharing. Some people
resort to lying or deceit, as when they carry two tins, the empty
one of which is displayed as proof that they have no tobacco.
People take puffs from other people's cigarettes, and wads of already chewed tobacco regularly pass from mouth to mouth, or
from behind the ear (where it is stored after initial chewing) to
mouth.

The mass media's effect on Jigalong Aborigines has so far
been minimal, in that very little reaches the mission, and most of
what does is ignored. Some younger adults who own radios listen
to musical programs featuring country and western songs, but
older people have no interest in nontraditional music. A few Aborigines sometimes listen to national and regional news broadcasts
and may pick up items of news about the desert area, which occasionally rates a mention.[4] The few comics, magazines, and newspapers that find their way into the Camp are rarely looked at, even
by younger literate Aborigines, unless they contain pictures. But
anything pictorial that pertains to Aborigines or Aboriginal culture
causes great interest. One Christmas, for instance, the pensioners'
gift parcels were wrapped in colored paper covered in Aboriginal
motifs, weapons, and hunters which was subject to close scrutiny
and prolonged discussion by a large group of men. The Aboriginal
men welcome such material, because they perceive it as proof of
the continued existence of Aboriginal culture in other parts of
Australia. They are fearful, however, that secret-sacred symbols,
objects, or activities will be depicted, because such things are considered extremely dangerous to women and the uninitiated. This
fear is evidenced in their distrust of cameras, partly because they
have seen photos of sacred objects in magazines, and also because
several years ago one of the missionaries betrayed them, they say,

---

[4]When I returned to the mission from a brief desert trip in November 1963 the
Aboriginal men told me that they had heard the news broadcasts of Presi-
dent Kennedy's death, and were quite worried because they thought that
Australia had been left without a "head boss."

by deliberately showing color slides of sacred objects (which the men had allowed him to film) to women and children.[5]

The initiated men also distrust movie films, especially after incidents at the mission in which films of Aboriginal secret-sacred dances were shown to an audience consisting mainly of children. During one show I was attending, there was a sudden uproar over a film concerning New Guinea tribal dances, when one of the older men mistook the headdresses of the dancers for Aboriginal thread-crosses and shouted to the women and children to cover their faces — which they did as they fled in panic from the hall.

In economic activities, where their dependence on whites is most noticeable, the Aborigines have readily accepted the practice of working in return for money or goods. This practice is merely a form of reciprocity, an intrinsic principle in their traditional value system. But few Aborigines conceive of employment as a means to accumulate capital for future use. They view work instead as a necessary subsistence strategy, and, if they are employed on stations, as a means of getting enough money to manage a short holiday in town or at the mission once the work is completed. Only a small minority of workers employed regularly at the same station manage to save enough money to purchase vehicles.

Although it is clear that the Aborigines have not embraced the Protestant work ethic, many view their work as more than a mere means to an end. Younger men, in particular, enjoy stock-work for its own sake because they love riding horses and motor-cycles and driving station vehicles. These young men have adopted many of the outer trappings of the "cowboy culture," as noted earlier, and their daily work as cowboys gives credence to this self-image. They have not, however, forsaken the traditional culture. While they are on stations, they enjoy emulating the cowboy image , but they are equally enthusiastic ritual participants when at the mission, and they evince great interest in the Law.

The Aborigines have had little difficulty in accepting the use of money, just as they have coped very well with the idea of employment. Only in recent years have they become accustomed to

---

5 I regret the absence of photographs of secret-sacred ritual activities and objects in this book, but I promised the Aboriginal elders that I would not publish photographs of a secret-sacred nature.

Plate 11. "Cowboy culture": young men wearing typical station clothing.

Plate 12. "Traditional culture": some of the same young initiated men fully decorated and waiting to participate in a ritual.

handling cash, but even illiterate adults are aware of the relative values of most denominations of currency, and know roughly how many goods, such as bags of flour, can be bought with how much money. However, the recent introduction of decimal currency (February 1966) has caused some initial problems for the Aborigines and for many white Australians as well.

Most money is used to purchase goods from the mission store, but at any given time there is usually a small amount circulating during gambling activities. If no moneyed newcomers arrive, the amount in circulation dwindles as it disappears into the store. Probably the only time that large amounts remain unused is after the collection of food money for the feasts that accompany circumcision and other rituals. A small minority of Aborigines have adopted gambling as a major spare time activity at the mission, and for them it may on occasion take precedence over religious matters. But it appears to be more important as a form of recreation than as a means of amassing sums of money for spending purposes. The appropriateness of this kind of recreation is questioned by the local initiated men only when it occurs during periods of ritual activity. At such times, the Aborigines — most of whom rarely gamble — perceive it as a threat to the Law, because it is "whitefella business" which had no place in the Dreamtime.

Attitudinal Changes

Of particular interest here is what is happening to the schoolchildren, because they have been singled out by the missionaries as the targets of determined attempts to replace one set of values with another. Success in converting the children to Christianity would undoubtedly spell disaster for the Aboriginal Law, which is based on a radically different view of life. The Law depends for its continuance on the successful indoctrination and initiation of its young Aborigines into the ways and the secrets of their elders who are the current Law custodians. Such is the fragility of orally transmitted cultural lore that in the space of one generation much can be irrevocably lost.

In the school and dormitories, the children are taught many aspects of Western culture, such as the three R's, personal hygiene, and "good manners." Back in the Camp situation, however, the children quickly discontinue most of the behaviors expected of them by the local whites. In some cases, this may be because it is not possible to practice them (for example, to eat with knife and fork), but in most cases it is because such behaviors are not considered by either the children or their parents to be worth observing. The children conform to what is expected of them in both the dormitory-school and Camp milieus to avoid undue conflict and possible punishment. This latter possibility is much less likely in the Camp because of their parents' extreme leniency. When the children finally are through with school and leave the dormitory, at age fourteen or fifteen, the sanctions that underlie most of the alien behavior patterns imposed on them by the whites are removed. The children adjust easily to Camp life on a full-time basis, and they soon abandon the missionary mantle. The only exceptions are the few teen-age girls who continue to live in dormitories and seek mission protection to prevent their marriage to men very much older than they. But, as was pointed out earlier, most of them eventually return to the Camp after becoming pregnant and are thus lost to the mission cause.

When they leave school, the children follow in large measure the cultural dictates of their elders. As young adults, they express a firm belief in the reality and truth of the Dreamtime and seek to emulate the rest of the community in following the Law.[6] There are now ample opportunities for young men to find employment on stations hundreds of miles from Jigalong, and to avoid having to return and face the harrowing ordeals of circumcision and subincision — yet so far not one young man has chosen this course of action. The young men return to face these trials because they know they must be initiated if they are to achieve social recognition as adults, marry, and become active participants in the religious life. The youths I talked to who were waiting to be initiated

---

[6] Cf. Meggitt, who says of the young Walbiri men of Central Australia: ". . . (they) are not yet prepared to break away from their own cultural background in order to attain a higher status. Thus. . . they do not overtly challenge the old institutions. Men who can drive motor-trucks, who buy gramophones with their earnings, who wear sandals, socks and sunglasses, still want to marry 'straight' and to learn their lodge mysteries. They still wish to 'follow the Walbiri line', a desire that in itself indicates the great vitality of that line." (1962:333)

were all quite anxious about what lay ahead, but at the same time were excitedly anticipating their entry into the men's secret religious life.

The viewpoints of the old and young at Jigalong are certainly not identical in all matters, and some intergeneration tensions exist. There is mutual dissatisfaction about certain behaviors. The older people feel that too many of the young are more interested in sex than the Law, while the young initiated men, who show considerable enthusiasm for ritual activities, complain that the elders are lethargic about organizing rituals, because they allegedly spend much of their time in endless discussion and argument. Despite these tensions, which sometimes surface as a result of particular incidents, there have been no major conflicts pitting the younger men against their elders, and both groups continue to share substantially similar value-orientations. Although they have readily adopted the cowboy image, the young men of Jigalong are not really more involved in Western culture than other members of the community, and most see a future for themselves that is little different from the present of most of their elders — except that the young hope to own vehicles, guitars, and radios.

The Aborigines' attitudes towards alien authority vary according to the category of whites who exercise it. The Aborigines accept the presence of the missionaries as long as these whites make no attempt to interfere actively in their religious life. In the case of government authority, the Aborigines understand little about the government, but they realize it is a powerful body, and that the police sometimes act to carry out its laws. They fear the police and dislike imprisonment because it involves confinement and separation from relatives, but not because it carries any social stigma. The Aborigines are indifferent to the white man's law unless the government attempts to enforce its laws by police action.

The Aborigines favor a live-and-let-live relationship with the government, but a fear persists among them that new laws will be passed to prohibit some of their traditional practices, particularly circumcision and subincision. Subincision is surrounded by such secrecy that the missionaries are unaware that the operation is still being performed. Periodically, rumors concerning new government laws sweep through the Camp and cause much discussion and worry. For their part, the Aborigines say that they are not interested in the white man's law — as long as it leaves their Law alone—

because it belongs to the whites and is for them, not Aborigines, to follow. In 1963, when visiting officials offered them the opportunity to vote in forthcoming statewide elections, the Aboriginal men had many discussions, then decided against accepting the offer. They felt such elections were not their concern, and they were frightened that they would vote, unknowingly, for someone who might be opposed to the Aboriginal Law.

News that "big government bosses" will be visiting the mission usually arouses great interest among adult men in the Camp. Some people put on clean clothes and others postpone hunting trips in the hope that they will be able to meet with the visitors. Such meetings rarely occur, however, because most government officials (with the exception of some Native Welfare officers and the local policeman) never go anywhere near the Camp and transact all their business with the missionaries.

The Aborigines have accepted the presence of whites without question and do not seem preoccupied with questions about having been dispossessed or exploited by the whites. The mission lies in what was originally the territory of the Njijabali people, so the Aborigines now at Jigalong are aware that they, as well as the whites, are immigrants to the area. However, they consider the mission holdings to be as much their territory as the missionaries' and are incensed whenever the missionaries evict young men accused of making trouble (most often with the older girls under the protection of the mission), or when the missionaries refuse to give them rides back from Meekatharra. The Aborigines are convinced that the missionaries paid for the mission truck with money withheld from the pensioners. Therefore, they reason, the truck belongs equally to them, and they have a right to ride in it. These and other aspects of missionary-Aborigine relationships are discussed in the following chapter.

Modifications Accompanying Acceptance

In acculturation situations, many elements borrowed by the recipient culture undergo some alteration in their form, meaning, or use in their new context. As Linton notes, the borrowing culture copies particular patterns of behavior, often without understanding their original cultural context, and it imbues them with

new meanings (1955:45). In the case of material goods, the Jigalong Aborigines have accepted many items for different purposes
from those originally intended. Wool, for example, is never used
for knitting, but is in great demand for other purposes. In fact, in
warmer months men sometimes unravel knitted garments to obtain
wool for making thread-crosses or for use as body decorations.
Similarly, handkerchiefs are used to make head-coverings, but never
for nose-blowing. Steel drill bits, properly filed down, are prized
as carving tools but not for their use in drilling holes.

The Aborigines do not question the alien origin of most of
the objects they now use. In fact, they take the technological
achievements of Western culture very much for granted. This attitude is at least partly a result of their firm conviction that the ancestral beings, as great magicians, possessed and utilized much of
this technology long before the whites acquired it. In the case of
several secret-sacred objects in the possession of some native doctors, it is obvious to an outside observer that these objects are of
Western manufacture, yet the Aborigines emphatically deny this.
These objects are of two kinds, cut-glass decanter stoppers and
radio tubes or bulbs of an uncommon type. Each is connected to
a length of hairstring by a wad of spinifex gum. When these objects were first revealed to me, amid great secrecy, the men stressed
that they had been left behind by the ancestral beings for use by
Aborigines and are definitely not "whitefella" things. The Aborigines call them *guṛu* 'eyes' and say that they use them to light
up the night sky for native doctors as they travel in dream-spirit
form to distant areas, carrying as passengers a group of Aborigines
who sit astride the hairstring (which in flight becomes a huge
snake). Although the men are correctly identifying the bulbs as
a source of light — and the cut-glass as a reflector of light — they
confidently deny that these objects are nontraditional because, it
seems, they have never seen such things in use among whites. They
acquired the objects from northern Aborigines, who also supplied
an explanation which validates their mythological origin. The
men were clearly aware that the objects looked manufactured, but
their belief in the magical powers of the Dreamtime beings is so
strong that they never doubted the truth of the accompanying
validation. The Aborigines' belief that the beings possessed much
of what the whites now possess indicates further the importance
of the traditional world view and of the way religious beliefs per-

meate their cognitive system. Also, this belief perhaps makes it easier for the Aborigines to accept the objects that they want. Such beliefs surely aid the Aborigines in absorbing certain aspects of their present condition into the eternal truths of the Dream-time.[7]

---

[7] For all this, the Aborigines, unlike many Melanesian people, do not seem to have taken this reasoning further, to enquire how it is that the whites now have the material wealth, yet the Aborigines do not, and then to respond to this dilemma by seeking access to the wealth through so-called Cargo Cult activities (cf. Burridge 1969). Cargo Cults have not been a feature of Aboriginal adjustment to the intrusion and dominance of whites.

CHAPTER SIX

Continuities and the
Rejection of Christianity

It has been emphasized that the social organization and religious life of the Aborigines at Jigalong reveal strong continuities with the traditional past. By designating these people as primarily tradition-oriented, I am suggesting that these continuities still outweigh the changes that have occurred as a result of the Aborigines' sedentarization as fringe dwellers.

The main reasons for this successful maintenance of traditional values and activities are not difficult to discern. The atypical history of culture contact in the Western Desert has undoubtedly helped the Aborigines in their adjustment to the presence of whites. The relatively isolated location of the mission and the very small white population in the Jigalong area are also relevant factors. Of greater significance is the fact that, outside the actual work situation, the few whites with whom adult Aborigines interact make little concerted effort to persuade them to adopt alien behavior patterns and values. From the vantage point of the outside observer, there is a clear element of choice in the reactions of the Aborigines to nontraditional cultural elements that confront them in the contact situation. Yet from the viewpoint of the Aborigines themselves, their choices are limited because they regard their continued conformity to the Law as a cultural imperative. They see their well-being as dependent upon continued reciprocity with the spiritual realm and the faithful following of the comprehensive life-design laid down for them in the Dreamtime. The acceptance of most Western material goods is not considered to be a threat, but to accept the white man's kinship system, or to embrace his attitudes towards status, wealth, thrift, the future, religion, or the good life would inevitably lead to conflict with traditional dictates.

With these factors in mind, it is now possible to focus on the nature of the relationship between the Aboriginal and missionary subcultures. The dominant aims, values, and aspirations of these two coresident groups are in most respects antithetical; and as a result, their members interact minimally across racial boundaries and with a considerable amount of mutual dislike and distrust.

Nowhere is the resistance of adult Aborigines to alien non-material cultural elements demonstrated more clearly than in their rejection of Christianity. Part of this rejection stems from the circumstances of culture contact in the Jigalong area, and part of the failure of the mission to win more than one firmly committed convert in twenty-four years is explicable in terms of certain fundamentalist values and attitudes held by the Apostolic missionaries.[1]

The Whitefella-Christian Dichotomy

Local Aborigines distinguish clearly between "whitefellas" and "Christians" partly as a result of the relatively recent intrusion of the Apostolic missionaries into the Jigalong area. Many of the adult Aborigines now at Jigalong experienced at least a decade or two of contact with frontier whites prior to the arrival of the missionaries, and in that time developed a fairly clear role-stereotype of those whites. When the missionaries arrived, the Aborigines were confronted by a group of whites whose behavior was strikingly different from that of the whites to whom the Aborigines had become accustomed. Through prolonged contact with the mission, the Aborigines developed a role-stereotype of missionaries as a special category of whites. So strong is the Aborigines'

---

[1] The comments which follow pertain specifically to the Jigalong situation. I am in no way inferring that other Australian missions or missionary subcultures share similar characteristics. I have not done prolonged research at any other missions and therefore cannot offer comparative comments. A body of literature on Australian missions exists, but few anthropologists have written at length on this topic. A recent article by Wolcott concerning the subculture of American missionaries in urban Africa reveals some interesting parallels with the Jigalong missionary subculture (1972:241-258).

association of "Christian" with the absence of smoking, drinking, swearing, blaspheming, and sexual joking, that they cannot believe that there are Christians who occasionally do some of these things. Thus if the Aborigines notice that a visiting white is smoking, he cannot, by definition, be a "Christian." Although I do not smoke, the possession of tobacco was sufficient to disqualify me from the "Christian" category.

Another important characteristic of the "Christian" category, and one that helps explain why Jigalong Aborigines have a negative attitude towards its incumbents, is that such people express a strong desire to change many aspects of the Aboriginal culture and are outspoken in their opposition to the Law, and especially to that part of it which concerns traditional religious activities. "Whitefellas," on the other hand, have always demanded certain responses to the work situation but have not interfered with the religious life and have not expressed any strong disapproval of it.

Characteristics of the Missionary Subculture

The Apostolic Church in Australia has had little experience in missionary work and, apart from Bible-study schools, it has no training facilities to prepare its missionary volunteers for the field. They arrive at Jigalong with their native skills and the ability to conduct prayer meetings, but they have no specialized missionary skills; they are untrained in linguistics, anthropology, or desert survival, and have little or no knowledge of Aboriginal culture.

The missionaries are of varied backgrounds — building contractor, mechanic, plumber's assistant, merchant seaman, nurse, housewife — but none of them is a highly educated professional. Only one has any prior experience in stockwork, yet the mission's principal nonevangelical activity is the running of stock as a commercial enterprise. Almost all the missionaries are suburbanites with no previous experience of desert living or of working with members of a non-Western culture. They have been somewhat isolated from the wider society by virture of their adherence to the Apostolic faith, which gives them whatever sense of unity they possess. They are not aggressive socially and tend to be ill at ease with strangers, preferring to avoid social contacts with them if possible, just as they try to avoid face-to-face conflicts with one another and with Aboriginal adults.

Their motives in coming to the mission can be assessed from two contrasting viewpoints, their own and that of the outside observer. They assert that they have come in answer to God's call, which summoned them to save the souls of the Aborigines by guiding them along the path of righteousness and grace to Apostolic Christianity. Their primary motive in devoting two or more years to missionary endeavor is clearly a religious one, and it is strongly felt. Few of them claim to be motivated primarily out of any deep and abiding love of their fellow man, and in view of their behavior and attitudes towards the local Aborigines (and also towards one another at times), it would be difficult to accept any such claims.

To the observer, several other motives seem pertinent. By coming to Jigalong these people are escaping from a society in which a majority of people are steeped in many "vices" that the Apostolics cannot tolerate or bear to witness: drinking, smoking, swearing, blaspheming, gambling, dancing, fornicating, wearing "indecent" clothing, breaking the sabbath, and failing to attend church. By retreating to Jigalong they free themselves from the daily trauma of confronting a multitude of offensive things. Also, through missionary work they assure themselves of personal salvation as well as increased esteem and higher status within the church hierarchy; returning missionaries are always heroes in the eyes of their home congregations. They believe that if they continue to pray and to accept Jesus Christ as their savior, they will gain their rightful place in heaven. Another possible motive in the case of some of the male missionaries is that by coming to Jigalong they are given positions of authority and power over Aborigines. For some this is the first opportunity to command others, and they obviously relish the chance to be assertive and to give orders.

The missionaries share a fundamentalist religious orientation; they believe in the literal interpretation of the Bible, they are totally opposed to evolutionary theory, they believe in the baptism of the Holy Spirit in its many manifestations, especially glossolalia (speaking in tongues), and the gifts of interpretation and prophecy. They believe that they are the chosen few, and their outlook is messianic; their prayers are aimed at inducing a massive outpouring of the Holy Spirit, which will usher in the new life and bring man dramatically to a realization of the truth and the power of the Almighty.[2] Man and his society are inherently evil and corrupt, so it is only through the power of intercessory prayer that they can induce God to transform both man and society into a state of grace. The exclusiveness of the missionaries manifests itself in their extremely negative opinions of most other sects, but particularly Roman Catholics and "high church" Anglicans, for whose elaborate ritualism they have nothing but contempt.

They view the Aborigines as the children of the devil, lost in the great darkness and steeped in sin. Aboriginal culture is thus the work of the devil and the antithesis of Christian virtues, principles, and behaviors. Syncretism of Aboriginal and Christian beliefs is therefore impossible; the Law must be destroyed and replaced with the Christian way of life. Because justice does not have to be ministered to the devil's people, acts such as the degrading and painful punishment of Aboriginal offenders, mainly children, are not considered cruel or unchristian, but rather are regarded as merciful acts performed for the recipients' ultimate good.

In addition, the missionaries hold steadfastly to the belief that the local Aborigines are low in intelligence, even when compared to Aborigines in other parts of Australia, and this helps them to rationalize their lack of success at Jigalong. Because of this low intelligence, the missionaries claim, it is impossible to teach the local Aborigines skills that have been successfully acquired by Aborigines in other missions. The missionaries often repeat the same kind of statement one sometimes hears from station whites: the Aborigines are like children and should be treated as such, firmly and paternalistically. Because few missionaries or local whites are aware of the complexities of Aboriginal culture, their beliefs in this regard are unshakeable.

---

2 Writing about Jigalong in the magazine of the Australian Apostolic Church, one of the female missionaries says, "How much we need a real 'break through' in Jigalong, a mightly deluge of the Spirit, the ministry of the miraculous to open the eyes of those lost in a great darkness" (1963:33).

The Dormitory System

The missionaries sometimes conduct prayer meetings aimed at the Aboriginal adults, but they in fact regard the adults as largely beyond redemption. They concentrate their greatest efforts on the more malleable schoolchildren. Apparently unaware of evidence from earlier experiments in other missions in Australia and overseas, the missionaries believe that by partially segregating the children in dormitories they can produce a generation of Christians who will reject the ways of their parents. The missionaries hope to achieve their aim through the heavy indoctrination of Christian theology and morality, supplemented by persistent warnings about the evils of the way of life of the adult Aborigines.

The Aboriginal children who enter the dormitory, however, have already experienced five or six years — the crucial formative period — of socialization in the Camp milieu, and throughout their school years they continue to have regular contact with their relatives in the Camp. The children grow up speaking the Aboriginal dialect as their first language, and they understand little about Christianity because it is presented to them in English, much of it Biblical. Under these circumstances, the children never become sufficiently alienated from the values of their relatives to reject the life of the Camp.

In the dormitory situation, the children must obey many rules, do daily chores, and attend all religious services or face possible physical punishment. Wrongdoers are beaten with straps or canes by the missionary in charge of their dormitory or by the superintendent himself. The children much prefer the indulgent treatment they receive from older relatives in the Camp, and because they are not used to chastisement, they are sometimes rebellious towards the missionaries. Such rebellion at times involves attempted retaliation by force, but more often results in children running away into the bush. When the older children stage their periodic breakouts from the locked dormitories at night, normal activities are suspended until the missionaries locate all the escapees and escort them back to the settlement.

As noted earlier, boys and girls are housed in separate dormitories, built at opposite ends of the mission to keep the sexes apart. One noticeable characteristic of the Jigalong missionaries is their apparent obsession with sex; they frequently discuss the alleged sexual depravity of the Aborigines, and they go to extreme lengths

Plate 13. Weekly prayer meeting is held beside the mission store before the pensioners receive their rations. The missionaries stand near the hospital verandah as they sing and clap. Note the spatial separation of the two groups and the absence of Aboriginal men.

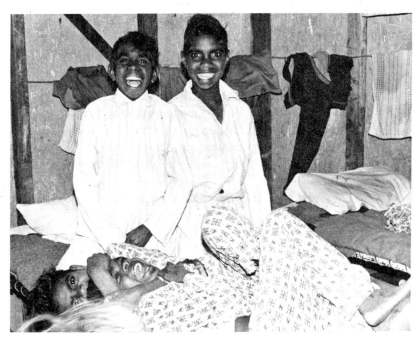

Plate 14. Schoolboys play in their dormitory before lights out at night.

to minimize the possibility of boys and girls coupling sexually. Older children show considerable interest in sexual matters and often talk to one another about their exploits with members of the opposite sex. There are more active manifestations of this interest, too, when they arrange secret meetings for the purpose of having intercourse. Since a great deal of missionary activity is aimed at preventing such occurrences, the consummation of sexual plans is a matter of some resourcefulness and daring, and the fact that young people sometimes succeed is a tribute to their determination.

Despite some opposition from the Aboriginal adults, the missionaries cling determinedly to the dormitory system, because its continued operation gives them a semblance of success in their endeavors at Jigalong. In the school-dormitory milieu the children conform to many non-Aboriginal behaviors, but most of this conformity is based on compulsion by alien authority. The fact that the children discontinue most alien behavior patterns when the underlying sanctions are not operating, as in the Camp situation, suggests that the dormitory system is not successful in achieving either its religious or secular aims.

Aboriginal-Missionary Interaction

The two main arenas of interaction are the Camp and the main settlement itself. But no matter where it occurs, most Aboriginal-missionary interaction is of a formal structured nature and implies differences in status and authority. Relaxed and informal interaction is rarely sustained between members of the two groups.

The missionaries have uniformly negative feelings about the Camp, which they see as a polluting influence on the children whose souls they are attempting to save. It is a place of "vice, sin, and filth," to quote the superintendent, so the missionaries rarely go there and they forbid their children to play there.[3] At times

---

[3] Nor do the missionaries like their children to play with the Aboriginal children. In the same magazine article mentioned in the preceding footnote, the missionary writes, "Among the many difficulties (sic) of this field is the very real problem of the children of the missionaries, not only the climate but the

the missionaries visit the Camp en masse to conduct brief prayer meetings, which are virtually ignored by the Aborigines. Otherwise, only the superintendent and the stock manager visit regularly, and they do so for a specific purpose, such as to pick up a sick or wounded person, to attempt to stop a fight, or to collect and deliver laborers. Less formal visits, when missionaries go there to photograph nonsecret ritual activities that are visible from their houses, are rare, partly because the Aborigines never invite them to attend. There are no close friendships between missionaries and adult Aborigines, and no reciprocal visiting occurs on this basis. Apart from housegirls and children doing chores, Aborigines do not enter missionaries' houses.[4]

More interaction takes place in the main settlement area than in the Camp, yet most of this is characteristically brief and confined to the business of the moment. At the clinic, store, and dining shed, where Aborigines and missionaries are in daily contact, communication tends to be minimal. The language barrier hinders communication, and neither side is really interested in prolonging the contact, unless there is something to complain about to the other. Aboriginal adults rarely initiate contacts unless they want something or are unhappy about some recent act of the missionaries. The missionaries express a liking for the aged Aborigines, who rarely cause them any trouble, and their interaction is superficial but generally amicable.

The Aborigines who have by far the most intensive contact with the missionaries are the housegirls who work five or six days a week as domestics. This closer contact has not resulted in the conversion of the women to the Apostolic faith, and it has not resulted in the creation of strong bonds of mutual affection between them and the female missionaries. The subordinate status of the Aboriginal women and the shortcomings the missionaries perceive in them prevent the establishment of egalitarian rapport. Despite

---

peculiar dangers and temptations arising from association with the native children...," and the writer goes on to request special prayers for these missionary children from the Australian congregations (1963:33).

[4] The only exceptions to this are the Christian Aboriginal stockman and his wife (whose wedding was mentioned in Chapter Two), who regularly attend prayer meetings in the houses of the missionaries.

this social distance, however, the missionaries sympathize with the Aboriginal women, whom they see as hapless victims of a cruel and repressive male chauvinist society, and in general their attitudes towards the women are more positive than those towards the Aboriginal males. Also, the women often attend the missionaries' prayer meetings and hymn sessions, "to make the poorfellas (missionaries) happy," they say, and because free tea and cookies are usually served. The Aboriginal men never participate in such "Christian law business," because they perceive it as opposed to their Law.

Communication Difficulties

Because the whites with whom they have contact cannot speak or understand more than a few Aboriginal words, most Aborigines have attempted to gain at least a limited command of English to communicate with them. The English they speak is modified by the influence of their own language, which lacks certain English sounds (such as those written s, sh, f, h, v, x) and does not distinguish between certain others (p and b, t and d, k and g). Their language has a very different grammatical structure and stress system; almost every word begins with a consonant and ends with a vowel, so the Aborigines transform most English words to fit this pattern. Thus, "ax" becomes *jagidji*, "reserve" becomes *re:djabu,* and so on. Because of these modifications, their spoken English is often quite difficult for whites to follow. English words have been incorporated into native speech, but they are few and are usually so transformed in rapid speech that they become unrecognizable from Aboriginal words.[5]

The adult Aborigines' limited command of English and the refusal of the missionaries to learn the Aboriginal language are only part of the problem of poor intercultural communication at Jigalong. Both parties seem to engage in the deliberate perpetuation of faulty communication because it has positive survival value for both and is thus a major strategy for coping with the present

---

[5] Since the schoolchildren are taught formal English daily during the school year and are forbidden to speak in the native dialect during school hours, they naturally acquire a better grasp of English than most of their parents.

situation. Both sides lack the desire to learn or understand more about each other's values, behaviors, and culture in general, and are content to retain their mutually negative stereotypes. The combination of antithetical value systems and the absence of informal channels of communication ensures a continuing lack of rapport between them. At present neither side is willing to make concessions or attempt to end the standoff.

The missionaries share a consistently negative stereotype of the adult Aborigines. Newly arrived missionaries quickly adopt the attitudes of their colleagues already at Jigalong and within a short time talk with conviction about the faults of the Aborigines: low intelligence, male cruelty, laziness, blatant lying, depraved sexual behavior, lack of hygiene, and complete lack of gratitude for goods and services rendered them. This attitude enables the missionaries to regard the adults as virtually beyond help or salvation (unless an outpouring of the Holy Spirit occurs) and justifies their continuing failure to either evangelize or "civilize" the adults.

Because the missionaries can remain at Jigalong only if they rationalize their failure and rid themselves of nagging self-doubt, their adaptive strategy is to blame the Aborigines for almost everything. For this reason they do not want to know more about the achievements of traditional desert culture, nor are they interested in stories of alleged missionary successes in other parts of Australia, because their negative stereotype of the Aborigines must not be shattered.

The missionaries are in a difficult position. In addition to pressures exerted by the local adults, there are worrisome external pressures. They must answer to the Apostolic Church authorities and congregations which lend financial support and expect not only saved souls, but also profit from the mission's pastoral activities. Their communications with the church must deal optimistically with chatty news of the missionaries and their health problems, and include constant references to the difficulties of living in the desert and dealing with Aborigines.[6] The government

---

[6] Cf. Wolcott, discussing communications between the American missionary in Africa and his congregation back home: "... his reports emphasize the picturesque, the exotic, the 'primitive,' and the needy..." and he "tells the folks back home what he believes they want to hear. And that helps perpetuate not only their subculture but his own" (1972:258).

pressures them also because it wants tangible evidence of progress in return for the considerable amount of money it spends at the mission. The missionaries also live with the knowledge that local whites oppose their activities and freely transmit their negativism to the Aborigines they employ.

The missionaries react to these pressures by blaming their lack of progress partly on these external sources. As the missionaries see it, the church authorities do not understand their special problems at Jigalong and often make unreasonable demands. The government does not give them enough funds to allow them to do a good job, and the local whites are constantly plotting against them and inciting the Aborigines to disobey them.

The superintendent adds another dimension in the assignation of blame, because he claims that constant internecine strife among certain missionaries causes him more headaches than do the Aborigines. Considerable interpersonal tension among the small group of missionaries (evinced by their cliques, gossip, tale-carrying, note-sending, and backbiting) is another important reason why they cling to the sense of unity created by their shared negative stereotype of the Aborigines. The missionaries' frequent sickness and subsequent retirement from the field are not simply a function of prolonged culture shock or failure to gain the friendship and respect of the Aborigines, but are in part reactions to much unresolved tension in their relationships with other missionaries. The Aborigines sense this tension and frequently contrast themselves, as "happy" people, with the "poorfella" missionaries, for whom they sometimes feel genuine sympathy. For the outsider who is caught in the middle of all this, it is ironic to see each group at times pitying the other, but for very different reasons.

Because of poor communication with the missionaries, the Aborigines' grasp of Christianity is fragmentary; they have a limited definition of "Christians" which contrasts with "whitefellas," but they are familiar with few tenets of the Christian religion. The missionaries preach in English, and they make few efforts to simplify or clarify their message as a concession to their Aboriginal audience. As one missionary admitted to me, less than five percent of a sermon would be understood by the adult Aborigines present. The Aborigines know about a "boss" called Jesus who lives in the sky, is everywhere yet invisible, and watches over Christians. But most adults are quite sceptical of his existence.

They would ask me, "This fella Jesus — you seen him?"; my negative answer was met with a knowing smile, signifying that if Jesus cannot be seen, he does not exist. They are aware that Jesus loves those who serve him and punishes those who sin against him. Most Aborigines have acquired some notion of what hell is, but they reject as nonsense the idea that spirits of the dead may be condemned there in afterlife if they have sinned. This contradicts their traditional belief that wrongdoing in this life is irrelevant to the course of the spirit after death, and that every spirit eventually returns to its place of origin.

The Aborigines see little connection between their religion and Apostolic Christianity. They say, therefore, that Christianity is for the "Christians" (but not for most of the whites they know) and the Law is for the Aborigines (cf. Meggitt 1962:331). Even if they wanted to, the missionaries lack the knowledge of Aboriginal cosmology necessary to refute it. Also, as Capell has noted, Aborigines are not likely to embrace a faith in which members of both sexes share the same body of religious knowledge and the same level of participation, because in Aboriginal culture women's status is definitely secondary and women must be excluded from the secrets of the men's religious life (1959:3).

The Aborigines are also disinterested in Christianity because it seems to prohibit smoking, swearing, drinking, sex, dancing, and having fun. Also, judging by the behavior of most of the missionaries, Christianity appears to lack values such as generosity, love, compassion, tolerance, and selflessness, all of which are important in Aboriginal culture. The irony is, of course, that these prime Aboriginal values have much in common with many in Christianity, but the local missionaries have failed to convey this similarity.

Besides a contented ignorance of Christianity, the Aborigines gain other advantages as a result of their poor communication with the missionaries. They are free to discuss any topic (including the missionaries themselves) in the presence of missionaries without the latter comprehending the conversation. They can thus exclude the whites, but the reverse does not apply as well because many Aborigines understand sufficient English to follow at least some of what is being said. The schoolchildren use the same technique to plan, in the presence of whites, what are often illegal activities.

More importantly, the Aborigines frequently take advantage of poor communication to ignore or to misunderstand deliberately requests or commands with which they do not want to comply. They are undoubtedly aided in this by their knowledge of the negative opinion the missionaries hold of them. Their persistent failure to understand will be viewed by the missionaries as further proof of their low intelligence, which reinforces the prejudices of the missionaries and at the same time absolves the Aborigines. The Aborigines benefit because they can work at minimal levels of exertion without constant chastisement for their poor performance, thus perpetuating the stereotype of themselves as dumb, lazy, and unreliable.[7] Since both sides gain distinct advantages from a continuance of faulty communication, neither attempts to improve the efficiency of the network that links them.

Aboriginal-Missionary Conflicts

If the term "accommodation," used in its sociological sense, is taken to mean the mutual adjustment of groups that retain their own identity and interests, then Aboriginal-missionary relationships at Jigalong suggest a situation of unstable accommodation in which interests remain to a large extent antagonistic, but a temporary adjustment occurs as the two groups adapt to immediate realities (cf. Broom and Selznick 1958:29). A symbiotic relationship exists between the Aborigines and missionaries to the extent that the Aborigines are the reason for the missionaries' presence and provide a labor source for the mission, and the Aborigines in turn depend in varying degrees on the missionaries for food and other material goods. The interdependence of the two groups forces them to coexist despite the continuance of unresolved issues and the ever-present feeling that disruptive changes could occur at any time.

Members of the two groups rarely clash physically or show overt antagonism, partly because they interact minimally, but also because the Aborigines know that if they assaulted a white, they would probably be put in jail. Yet the frequent expressions of dislike that one hears from both parties indicate that their con-

---

[7]This is a perfect example of what Merton has termed "self-fulfilling prophecy" (1957:423).

junctive relations are infused with a strong element of conflict-orientation. Both sides feel that they have good reasons for their antagonisms and will readily voice their grievances.

Although a number of specific incidents led to the Aborigines' decision to stage a walkout from the mission in 1962, it resulted also from their growing dissatisfaction with the missionaries and a greater awareness of the extent of their incompatibility. The conflict associated with the walkout and its aftermath brought the tensions between the two groups into the open for a time, and itself created further tensions. Observing the desperate efforts made by the missionaries to secure the return of the pensioners and schoolchildren, the adult Aborigines realized the vulnerability of the mission when faced with the loss of its inhabitants. On several occasions since, some parents have threatened to remove their children from the dormitories; the missionaries have dissuaded them by threatening outside intervention but are apprehensive nonetheless that the Aborigines may again evacuate the mission.

The missionaries' treatment of the children frequently arouses the ire of the Aborigines, especially when it involves corporal punishment. When parents learn that their child has been beaten, they arm themselves and hurry across to the settlement to confront the punisher. Blows are seldom struck, but the parents always make their objections known because they rarely ever hit their children and will fight any other Aborigine who does so.

The mission's policy of protecting older girls remains a major unresolved issue. While housed in their special dormitory, these girls are trained as domestics and receive religious instruction, and they are strongly encouraged by the missionaries to reject the men to whom they are betrothed. Both the Aboriginal parents and the prospective husbands object openly to this policy, maintaining that if the girls are living in Camp with their parents or husbands they can be properly supervised and prevented from running about with young men. When the girls break out periodically, they are soon caught and punished by the missionaries, and the beatings and subsequent detention of the girls angers both them and their parents. But several girls are generally happy with the arrangement because they do not want the men to whom they have been betrothed. These are the girls who also profess a belief in Christianity.

Money is another major point of contention, because the Aborigines believe that the missionaries are "hungry for money" and are robbing them of their due. Aborigines are convinced that the bulk of the pension payments withheld by the missionaries are used by the mission for its own purposes, which include the purchase of vehicles. Thus the Aborigines become very angry when the missionaries at times deny them rides in these vehicles. The meager wages paid by the mission cause much adverse comment among the Aboriginal employees. They are not told how much they are earning per week and never see any money unless they leave to go elsewhere — so they are sure they are being cheated. Female workers complain that fifty cents per week is little better than no wage at all. The missionaries, on the other hand, regard this payment as mere pocket money, because they feed and clothe the workers. The high markups in the mission store rarely draw comments from the Aborigines, because few of them have the opportunity to compare mission prices with those elsewhere.

The resentment of the Aborigines concerning the small amount of pension money paid out is also directed against the general treatment of the pensioners. They base their complaints about the inadequacy of the pensioners' diet and possessions on a comparison of the town-dwelling pensioners with those at Jigalong. The old people in the towns receive full pension payments and administer their own money, so most of them own more and eat better, according to the Aborigines at the mission. The Aborigines complain to government officials, which in turn sometimes leads to friction between the officials and the missionaries. The Aborigines also complain about a variety of other matters to the Native Welfare officers, hoping to discredit the missionaries. This ploy is rarely successful, however, so the Aborigines tend to view the officers as supporters of the whites rather than of those they are paid to assist.

The Aboriginal men dislike the superintendent's practice of intervening in Camp fights. The conflict usually ceases after the arrival of missionaries at the scene, but it is resumed as soon as the whites have departed. Aborigines consider Camp fights their own concern exclusively, to be settled as they think fit. They are incensed when the missionaries inform the police about what the combatants consider to be minor spear wounds, especially when the Aboriginal community considers the victim to be clearly in the wrong. When the police intervene and take away men who have been punishing a wrong-doer for the community's sake, the Aborigines are understandably outraged, and they tend to blame the missionaries for acting as informers.

The missionaries' opposition to the adult Aborigines stems mainly from the strength of their religious convictions. It is inevitable that the missionaries should regard the adults as the main obstacle to their successful conversion of the children, be-cause they see the adults as "steeped in the powers of the dark-ness" and given to vice and sin, an ever-present "bad example." The missionaries have only a vague idea of what transpires in Camp, and because much of their information is obtained from a few older girls, it is incomplete and selective. These girls are well aware of the kind of things that the missionaries like to hear, so they feed them with accounts of alleged depravity or brutality. This information is welcomed and accepted as the ab-solute truth. It is then repeated among the other missionaries and told to other whites in illustration of "just what kind of people these Aborigines really are." The missionaries also enjoy telling humorous anecdotes that depict Aborigines as childish or lacking in common sense. Accounts of wife-beating are eagerly received, because they confirm the missionaries' perception of Aboriginal men as immoral sadists who treat their wives as chattels.

The missionaries express strong resentment as what they con-sider are constant and unreasonable demands made upon them by adults of both sexes, who request goods and services yet never ex-press gratitude when their demands are met. The fact that there was no place for expressions of gratitude in the traditional culture, with its continuous reciprocity, means little to them, because they maintain that the Aborigines make no effort to conform to alien behavior patterns of which they are well aware. Therefore, this logic runs, the Aborigines "know right from wrong" and they must "do something about lifting themselves." The refusal of the Ab-origines to conform as desired is attributed to their laziness, stub-bornness, and desire to antagonize the missionaries. If this *is* the in-tention of the Aborigines, they succeed handily!

The Reinforcing Role of Tradition-Orientation

Much of the Aborigines' resistance to Christianity stems from their dislike of the missionaries who advocate it. The Aborigines consider only one of the local missionaries, the stock manager, to be a fair and good man; they respect him for his general ability, friendliness, and willingness to sit and chat informally with them. The Aborigines contrast him with the other missionaries who seem aloof and incapable of talking openly or of listening to what the Aborigines have to tell them. Yet, even if all the missionaries were liked, it cannot be assumed that conversion to Christianity would eventually follow. According to the Aborigines, some of the earlier missionaries were approachable and friendly but had no more success in gaining converts than those now at the mission. Regardless of individual virtues, some basic differences persist as long as the missionaries attempt to carry out their evangelical tasks and the Aborigines maintain their adherence to the major tenets of the Law.

In their dominant values the Jigalong Aborigines remain conservative. The "good" Aborigine is defined in terms of his conformity to relevant traditional values, which can be summed up as "holding on to the Law." The men exhort novices to be good Law-carriers and stress repeatedly the necessity of following the Law. The Aborigines maintain that the Aboriginal way is better for them than that of the whites, and they consider whites inferior to themselves in some respects. Aborigines do not seem to talk about whites much, but when they do, men often refer to white males as *barabunadja* 'unsubincised' and say that they are only "half-men" because of this. This attitude reflects the strongly held notion among Aborigines that manhood cannot be achieved in their society until a male is subincised.[8]

It has been noted that the traditional social organization is still largely intact, sanctioned as it is by the Dreamtime. The Aborigines' strong sense of mutual obligation and reciprocity, articulated in kinship terms, enables any community member to receive support when necessary. The continuing emphasis on sharing is somewhat incompatible with alien trends towards individuation

---

[8] Having been admitted to the men's secret life at Jigalong, I am often threatened with this operation by the adult men, on the grounds that it would complete my initiation. So far I have avoided the issue by claiming that subincision would probably kill a poor weak white man. In one sense, then, the Aborigines too have failed to gain a convert.

and competition, but the Aborigines see no advantage gained by accepting features of the Western system at the expense of their own. Alien practices such as the free choice of marriage partner, enforced monogamy, the tendency to restrict kinship to a narrow circle of relatives, and worshipful religion are viewed as pointless behaviors by the Aborigines.

The aspect of Aboriginal culture which most clearly reinforces their tradition-orientation is the religious life. Ritual activities, the transmission of religious lore, dream-spirit journeys, the finding, contemplation, and construction of sacred objects, the telling of myths, and the singing of songlines — all of these things affirm for the Aborigines the reality and relevance of the Dreamtime and its ancestral beings. Through ritual the Aborigines demonstrate their sense of responsibility towards the ancestral beings, their older revered kinsmen who have kinsmen's interests in the welfare of their human descendants and are therefore amenable to gestures of reciprocity. As long as the Aborigines continue to believe that their survival depends upon their retention of the Law, and specifically upon their regular performance of ritual, then the question of their possible acceptance of Christianity can never even arise.

One of the most ironic aspects of this situation of contact is the fact that the mission, unwittingly and indirectly, has facilitated the retention of the Law and its focal manifestation, the religious life. By allowing large numbers of tradition-oriented Aborigines to congregate on a permanent basis at Jigalong, the mission has enabled them to pool their religious knowledge and has given them ample spare time to devote to religious discussion and activity. This has resulted in an intensification of the Aborigines' religious as well as secular life, such that one writer has referred to Jigalong as "the mission that fostered tribal custom" (Fink n.d.).

Mention should be made here of the many striking similarities that exist between the missionary community at Jigalong and what has been termed the "station community," a common phenomenon in developing countries where small groups of Westerners are living in rural areas and assist with various programs aimed at improving social and economic conditions among the local inhabitants. The following quotations from a description of the characteristics of the station community should suffice to show how well Jigalong fits this category:

. . . station personnel and their families. . . tend to form a distinct social enclave. . . . They never do get around to the intimate observation of, and participation in, the client community's affairs that success in their work requires. Their efforts to learn the local language make little progress because they are not in a situation where they have to use it constantly. Their social relationships are established primarily with other members of the station community, so that they assimilate its dominant attitudes and conventions, including its stereotypes regarding the client community. . . . a station community of even a few families inevitably becomes a separate social world built on the common cultural background of its members, and to the extent that it does so it becomes cut off from the client community. . . . Station communities. . . are, in fact, notoriously insular. Their members have dealings with their administrative clients in such narrowly limited contexts, either on official business or as masters to domestic servants, that they may be almost totally ignorant of the language and culture of their clients after years of residence among them. (Goodenough 1963:413-415)

CHAPTER SEVEN

Conclusion: Strategies for Survival

The broad concern of this study is with social and cultural changes that have occurred among Aborigines as a result of contact with whites, but its specific focus is on the persistence of certain major continuities that link these Aborigines with their traditional heritage. Continuities are emphasized because the tradition-orientation of the Jigalong Aborigines is matched by few other Aboriginal communities in Australia. This fact makes it imperative to attempt to answer the inevitable question: how has this particular group of Aborigines been able to deal so successfully with the presence and pressures of a powerful alien culture? In dealing with this question, it will be necessary to recapitulate certain points made earlier, but this chapter is not meant to be merely a summary; its concluding section is devoted to a discussion of recent developments at Jigalong and to some suggestions concerning possibilities for the future.

The Emergence of the Jigalong Mob

Assuming that the strongly felt sense of community among Jigalong Aborigines is an important factor in the effectiveness of their adaptation to external pressures, it is necessary to examine the bases of community integration. It was noted earlier that the Jigalong community is a new type of social grouping for the Aborigines that has arisen in response to their migration from the desert and their sedentarization in a different physical and social environment. This grouping is much larger than the traditional hordes or local groups and is composed of members of linguistic groups from such widely separated territories that many of them never met one another traditionally, even at their periodic "big meetings." Yet when the Aborigines gathered at Jigalong and eventually became permanent coresidents, the basis for their future sense of group solidarity already existed. They were all members of the same cultural bloc, so they shared the same basic Law, regardless of any dialectal and subcultural differences. Their system of classificatory kinship reckoning made relatives of everyone, regardless of area of origin. Naturally, the old loyalties and the suspicion of those who had once been considered strangers lingered on, as did the potential for conflicts and schisms when disputing individuals engaged the support of their close kin. But over time and with the growing realization of a common "Aboriginality" distinct from the whites, the strength of these unifying pressures increased.

There has been a steady increase in intermarriage between members of different linguistic groups and a strong tendency towards settlement endogamy, because most men can obtain wives without going elsewhere. This has led to the development of many affinal bonds between coresidents and an associated web of reciprocity, which crosscut linguistic divisions and make it increasingly difficult for people to oppose one another readily on the basis of precontact loyalties. Since all at Jigalong are immigrants, they share a new home territory to which no one group has exclusive rights. For many of the younger people Jigalong *is* their home, in the sense of being their birthplace and the only territory they know.

The gradual emergence of the Jigalong mob, a self-conscious entity with considerable solidarity and ethnocentrism, can also be attributed to the relationships of its members with other fringe-area communities and to different levels of acculturation in different areas of the Western Desert periphery. People identify themselves as members of the Jigalong mob not merely as a convenient label when they travel or as a designation to be used by employers. The Aborigines have pride in their membership and enjoy Jigalong's reputation among whites and Aborigines alike as a very strong Law center.

The strength of community sentiment at Jigalong is best explained in terms of the Aborigines' shared Law, particularly in the aspects of kinship, world view, and religious life, the major integrating force. Above all else, the Aborigines' participation in ritual activity, which transcends all potentially disruptive divisions and demands that people be at peace, dramatically affirms the unity of the Aborigines and their unique cultural heritage. This heritage sets them apart from all whites and from Aborigines in other areas who have turned away from the Law. The successful creation and performance of rituals requires a great deal of cooperation among those who participate, and this reinforces community solidarity. Leadership structure, which was localized and situationally defined in the traditional society, has not been a suitable locus of community integration in the contact situation, so the new entity emphasizes its unity through ritual activities.

It should be clear from the discussion of the religious life at Jigalong that it has many positive functions for the community in addition to promoting solidarity. Rituals provide entertainment to vary the relatively monotonous routine of Camp life, and they necessitate a peaceful atmosphere. The threat of exclusion from ritual activities helps to discourage wrongdoing, especially among the men. All rituals have important educational and initiatory aspects, because they are major vehicles for the transmission of religious elements of the Law both within and between Aboriginal communities.

Active involvement in the religious life also has significant effects on Aborigines as individuals.[1] Although it is not possible to elaborate here, an Aborigine's participation in ritual activity involves processes of change, learning, and an increase in self-awareness that result from entry into the spiritual realm.[2] Close contact with the spiritual dimension of the cosmic order is always a temporary occurrence during an individual's lifetime, but it can

---

[1] While it is difficult to assess levels of individual religious commitment, I should point out that all able-bodied Jigalong men and women (with the exception of the Christian wife of the mission stockman's Aboriginal assistant) participate in the religious life.

[2] These processes are discussed in detail in my doctoral thesis (Tonkinson 1972:200-216).

be achieved through singing, dancing, contemplation of sacred objects, or dream-spirit experiences.

From their participation in the religious life the Aborigines gain many things including enjoyment, satisfaction, and a sense of control over their own destiny. But it is ritual, above all, that embodies the core of their Law. This shared agreement about the central importance of ritual and the maintenance of the Law integrates the community and unifies the Jigalong mob.

Coping with the Whites

Several background factors have been shown as relevant to the Aborigines' success in adapting to the contact situation, so only brief allusion need be made to them here: the atypical contact situation, which gave the Aborigines an initial element of choice in their dealing with whites; the marginal nature of the Western Desert, which prevented whites from settling in large numbers; the numerical superiority of the Aborigines; and the evolution of mutually beneficial Aboriginal-white relationships which resulted in a peaceful frontier. All of these factors have contributed significantly to the stability of the contact situation at Jigalong.

Also of importance is the relative recency of the Aborigines' immigration to Jigalong, which undoubtedly helps explain the persistence of continuities in their culture. The arrival of large numbers of the now numerically dominant Mandjildjara-speakers in the 1940s and 1950s resulted in the infusion of many new rituals into the religious life already functioning at Jigalong and added strength to traditional elements in the contact situation.

Jigalong's position as one of the most isolated communities in the Western Desert fringe area is clearly an important factor in the Aborigines' adaptation. Because of their isolation, Jigalong's Aborigines are subject to less acculturative pressures from the wider society than are neighboring Law centers, especially those in or near towns. Casual white visitors to Jigalong are rare, and for most government officials, Jigalong is a place to be visited only when absolutely necessary. If they are staying overnight, officials usually prefer to camp at neighboring stations, where their white hosts are generally more relaxed than the missionaries and serve cold beer.

Most Jigalong adults have traveled in the surrounding areas at some stage and are thus aware of what is happening among town-dwelling Aborigines, whose lives seem to be dominated by drunkenness, fighting, and gambling, with a consequent breakdown in the Law. Back in the isolation and relative peace of the mission, the Aborigines discuss what they have seen and say that the absence of liquor at Jigalong is a good thing. While not denying that they often drink and gamble in town, they condemn such activities in retrospect for making people's heads "no good" and causing them to neglect their families and the Law. The Aborigines are quite explicit about the advantages of living in an out-of-the-way place like the mission. They tell stories of theft and vandalism of sacred boards from unprotected storehouses near towns, and appreciate the fact that their own storehouses are safe from acquisitive whites. Not even the missionaries dare venture anywhere into "men's country" near the Camp.

It has been noted that neither visiting whites nor local missionaries spend much time in the Camp at Jigalong. This avoidance of the Camp, combined with the laissez-faire policy regarding the activities of Aborigines outside the work situation, enable the Aborigines to feel that they still control their own internal affairs and are free to carry on their ritual activities and kin behaviors.

This seemingly autonomous control is illusory because government decree could put an end to their present way of life at any time; so far, however, this has not happened. Outside intervention has been minimal and manageable, so the Aborigines have a pragmatic and realistic basis for feeling that as long as they remain at the mission and follow the dictates of the Law, they control the powers of self-regulation. They do in fact largely govern themselves and make their own decisions in what are to them the most meaningful aspects of their life. They have taken care to exclude almost all whites from witnessing most of their ritual activities, especially those that are secret-sacred to the initiated. Most whites they know are not interested in such matters or are ignorant of their meaning and significance to the Aborigines, or both, so the Aborigines have not had to contend with many attempts by outsiders to gate-crash the religious life.

It is in connection with economic matters that the Aborigines have the most interaction with whites, having been forced to settle for some kind of permanent association by their decision not to return to their former desert life. By working for whites and by receiving welfare benefits, the Aborigines can satisfy most basic wants, such as food, and most of their newly acquired needs, especially for material goods. The nature of pastoral employment is mutually beneficial. Graziers have a seasonal demand for the bulk of their labor force, so they employ Aborigines on a temporary basis to avoid paying for labor which they cannot use. This suits the Aborigines very well because they dislike remaining isolated on stations for long periods.

Mutual exploitation is also a pronounced feature of the employment scene. Whites tend to pay as little as possible and in kind rather than cash, and Aboriginal employees try to expend as little effort as possible, since they do not value secular work for its own sake, but merely as the means to satisfy their wants. Their attitudes towards work are also affected by the nature of frontier relationships on many stations in the Jigalong area. Many station whites have been prepared to accept the presence of nonproductive male employees if the wives or adult daughters of these men are employable as domestics or will act as sexual partners. The Aborigines have no moral qualms about this, and the men can tolerate the extra privileges and higher status of their women in the eyes of the white men because they receive food, clothing, and tobacco without expending much effort themselves.

Many younger Aboriginal men are often enthusiastic workers in activities relating to stockhandling, but in more mundane tasks they are disinterested and work fitfully. As noted in the previous chapter, the self-fulfilling prophecy of the Aborigines' laziness is particularly effective at the mission because of the missionaries' strong antipathy to the Aboriginal adults, especially as workers. This attitude towards work makes much sense to the Aborigines, for as Stanner has pointed out, "There is a sound calculus of cost and gain in preferring a belly regularly if only partly filled for an output of work that can be steadily scaled down" (1960:70). At the mission this is more than a matter of getting enough to eat, because employment enables many adults to remain near their school-age children and to participate in Law activities.

This situation has been characterized as a major phase in the postcontact adaptation of Aborigines everywhere. Elkin terms it "intelligent parasitism" and considers it an important but transitory strategy that Aborigines use to cope with whites (1951:164-186). Berndt prefers to consider this strategy as "the exploitation of all the available avenues through which a livelihood can be obtained," once the Aborigines have accepted the presence of whites as a permanent feature of their environment (1957:77). Jigalong is a good example of this phase of contact, an ongoing process in which the Aborigines are successful in extracting much from the whites while at the same time ignoring Christianity and running their internal affairs with a minimum of outside interference.

Because of their isolation, numerical ascendancy, and symbiotic relationship with local whites, the Jigalong Aborigines have not been subject to the overt prejudice that has inculcated strong inferiority feelings among Aborigines in many other parts of Australia. The Aborigines of Jigalong do not perceive whites en masse as prejudiced against them. They judge individual whites according to the circumstances of their interaction, except for the missionaries whom they tend to lump together into the negatively perceived category of "Christian." The weight of tradition encourages them to affirm their belief in the superiority of the Law. They accept Western material goods because such acceptance does not contravene the Law, but they firmly reject many nonmaterial alien elements that they consider to be antithetical to core aspects of the traditional culture and the means of its perpetuation. Their ethnocentrism prevents them from examining Western nonmaterial culture as a possible alternative to their own.

The Aborigines are sceptical of the ability of whites to communicate with and benefit from the spiritual realm. They scoff at such things as the missionaries' claims that Jesus brings rain in response to Christian prayer, because they believe that only Aborigines have the power to bring rain. When they walked off the mission in 1962, the Aborigines angrily told the missionaries that no more rainmaking would take place on mission property, so if the missionaries wanted rain they could pray to their Jesus and see how they fared. As it happened, no rain fell. When the Aborigines returned a few months later, they informed the missionaries that since Jesus had not brought rain, they would perform the rainmaking ritual and end the drought. Rain fell shortly after the ritual ended. Nothing would convince a Jigalong Aborigine that whites can bring rain.

The ethnocentrism of the Jigalong Aborigines is directed not only at whites but also at Aborigines in other areas whom they see disregarding the Law. Members of the Jigalong mob firmly believe that theirs is the only community of Aborigines which is still "holding onto the Law properly" and resisting attempts to modify or to weaken it. It was noted earlier that the Jigalong elders reacted quite negatively to their northern neighbors who attempted to institute a "new Law." Their resistance to the introduction of similar changes at Jigalong widened the ideological rift between them and the northern Aborigines. Intercommunity contact and cultural transmission continue along the desert periphery, but the Jigalong people are convinced that their Law is now the strongest. Their awareness of developments in the towns has not actually alienated them from their neighbors because strong kinship, friendship, and religious ties remain, but it does lead the Jigalong Aborigines to believe that they are coping far more effectively with the whites than are their town-dwelling neighbors.

Jigalong Aborigines would not deny that many changes have taken place as a result of their immigration to the settlement, and that these changes have led to some modification in their traditional behaviors. They have adapted to the new environment by capitulating to whites only when necessary and to avoid possible police intervention, but they disregard alien laws that are not policed. In spite of the inevitable changes, their traditional values remain a potent conservative force. Their firm rejection of Christianity, which in its Apostolic version (and judged according to the behavior of the missionaries) is at variance with the Law, attests to their continuing belief in the rightness of the Dreamtime heritage.

The Law as Defense: A Major Adaptive Strategy

It has been suggested that when traditional religious values and cosmological beliefs underlying an indigenous legal system are surrounded by a dominant alien culture, their retention constitutes a defense against possible social anomie, loss of cultural integrity, and total disruption of political cohesion (Tonkinson 1966:23). At Jigalong, the Law maintains and reinforces Aboriginal group-solidarity and cultural identity in the face of pressures towards change exerted by agents of the politically dominant Australian-European culture and also by more acculturated Aborigines in neighboring areas. This is why the Jigalong Aborigines are so adamant about the necessity of maintaining their Law. To a certain extent, theirs is the reaction of a conservative people to some kinds of innovation, but this is not sufficient to explain their attitude, for the Aborigines are also concerned with the possible erosion of what political integrity they have managed to retain in the contact situation. The adults perceive the Law as the last remaining repository of independent political action and maneuver.

As long as the Jigalong Aborigines continue to associate their well-being with the observance of the Law, they will resist attempts by whites and Aborigines from other areas to persuade them to compromise, and they will be wary of activities that they perceive as threatening the Law. From the outsider's viewpoint, the judgment of the Aborigines in this matter seems entirely correct, because their self-esteem lies in their possession and pursuit of a distinctive set of beliefs and practices. Abandonment of the Law would inevitably bring about a loss of the self-esteem necessary for survival as a viable cultural minority. The Aborigines have seen no examples of their fellows succeeding in the wider society, and nothing in their past experience and present situation suggests that this could even be a future possibility. In other words, they see no good alternatives to the Law, only the certainty of a numbing preoccupation with drinking, fighting, and gambling.

Although the Aborigines themselves may not regard retention of the Law as an actual strategy, the survival function of the Law is clear to an outside observer who compares and contrasts Jigalong with other Aboriginal-white contact situations. The Aborigines of Jigalong have adapted well to their new environment largely because their shared Law has welded them into an ethnocentric unity. The more acculturated Aborigines who live near towns have not adapted so well to their new milieu because they have relegated the Law to a secondary status in order to embrace gambling and drinking as primary pursuits, with disastrous consequences for their dignity and self-esteem.

Recent Developments and Future Possibilities

The conditions described in the previous chapter still obtained at Jigalong at the end of 1966. The missionaries' major adaptive strategy, blaming the Aborigines for whatever lack of progress existed, was working well and kept them from undergoing crises of conscience concerning their failure to save Aboriginal souls. But there was a major flaw in their strategy. They often punished Aboriginal children of both sexes by beating them, sometimes severely. In their fervent religiosity they had no qualms about this because children of the devil need firm guidance. It was a matter of teaching obedience and of attempting to beat some of the sinfulness out of them. As the missionaries saw it, such punishment was perfectly justified and would ultimately benefit the recipients. They perhaps failed to appreciate that if their treatment of the children was ever made public, government officials and other Australians would not view such punishment in a similar light.

The two state government employees who taught at Jigalong in 1965 and 1966 were not Apostolics and were not in sympathy with much that they witnessed while there, especially the use of corporal punishment for seemingly minor infractions, such as failure to attend Sunday school. Shortly after their return to Perth at the end of their tour of duty at Jigalong, they informed the news media that the superintendent had imprisoned and severely caned young Aboriginal girls for trivial offences. Early in 1967, amid great public outcry and nationwide publicity, police and Native Welfare officials investigated and proved the charges. The welts on one nine-year-old girl's legs were still visible more than three months after the caning. Senior church officials came from Melbourne and vehemently denied that what had happened was anything more than an unfortunate isolated incident. The superintendent, long disliked by the Aborigines, resigned shortly after.

After a flurry of articles and letters to editors in Perth newspapers, the incident was forgotten by the press and the public, and a period of relative calm followed at Jigalong. The missionary who was liked by the Aborigines took over as superintendent, and tensions between the Aborigines and missionaries eased somewhat. But the mission never really recovered from the blow of such adverse publicity. It was now an embarrassment to the church, which had trouble recruiting new staff as a result of the scandal. Persistent staff shortages led eventually to the closing of the dormitories which, in the eyes of the church authorities, meant the loss of the children on whom they had pinned their hopes. By 1969 the church was ready to listen to the suggestion that the Native Welfare Department take over the entire concern. The mission ceased operations on December 31, 1969, and the settlement became known as the Jigalong Aborigines Project, a government-run concern. The local Aborigines regarded the demise of the mission as a victory for the power of the Law. At the time of the government take-over, many men told me that the Law was too strong for the "Christians"; they were obviously delighted about this development and from it they gained a great deal of satisfaction and reassurance.

When I left Jigalong early in 1970, the Aborigines seemed pleased with the new administration, but were unsure about what they could expect from the government in the future. There were plans afoot to move the entire settlement to a far better site closer to the main highway, so the Aborigines were busily discussing the pros and cons of this proposal. To date, however, no such relocation has taken place.

As in any situation of change, it is difficult to make definitive statements about the prospects of a continued status quo at Jigalong. If the new administration maintains its policy of minimum interference in the internal politics of the Aboriginal community and religious life, and if it continues to ban alcoholic drinks from the settlement, conditions could conceivably remain much as they are for some years to come. Once the older Aborigines are gone, those who are now schoolchildren may become more deeply involved in the wider society, especially if they are sent to distant schools for higher education. This has not happened yet, nor has there been any migration of young adults to towns. The younger adults continue to follow most of the Law's major dictates and are avid participants in ritual activities.

Two relatively recent developments may be harbingers of change for the Jigalong people. At the end of 1968, minimum wage regulations became applicable to Aboriginal station workers. Since then, job openings on stations appear to have declined in number, because graziers claimed that they could no longer employ large numbers of Aborigines if they had to pay them full wages. A continuation of this trend could have disatrous effects on Aboriginal efforts to be economically self-sufficient. The other significant development was the establishment of a township and gigantic iron-ore mining operation at Mount Newman, about 100 miles west of Jigalong. At one stage a few Jigalong men were employed there as laborers, but by 1970 the mining company was making quiet efforts to rid itself of both Aboriginal employees and the small group of local Aborigines who were living on the edge of the town. Local police were telling Aborigines that they were not welcome in Newman.

Should large mineral deposits be found in the immediate vicinity of Jigalong and attract large numbers of whites for a prolonged period, a rapid breakdown of the Law could result, especially if the whites had open access to the settlement and liquor were readily available to the Aborigines. This, however, would necessitate a change in the status of Jigalong as a Native Reserve, and although in the past there have been cases of such reserves having portions reclassified following discoveries of minerals, such an act today would undoubtedly give rise to loud protests by civil rights groups. These groups, which operate in the large cities, have become very active in opposing any further alienation of reserve lands.

So far the great strength of the Jigalong people has been their pride in their Aboriginal identity and their Law, which has shielded them from the development of an inferiority complex. Judging by the situation of change in the Western Desert generally, Jigalong appears to be the community that has had the greatest success in maintaining its tradition-orientation with respect to its kinship system and religious life. It could well become the last bastion of traditional religion and culture in the Western Desert, should the flow of intercommunity cultural transmission lessen and eventually cease entirely as Aborigines experiencing more intense contact with the wider society abandon the Law.

After many decades of virtually ignoring the existence of the Aborigines, the Australian public has in the past few years undergone an awakening of conscience concerning the Aboriginal "problem." The old image of the Aborigines as a dying race is being replaced as whites become aware of the rapid growth rate of the Aboriginal population, which is expected to exceed 200,000 by the early 1980s (Jones 1970:37). The public is beginning to recognize the pressing need to allocate much more money for improving the socioeconomic position of the Aborigines in the wider society. Well-educated young Aborigines with great leadership potential are emerging, and rumblings of Black Power are being heard as a response to such things as deplorable living conditions, mistreatment, neglect, and the absence of Aboriginal land rights.[3] But the Australian public remains abysmally ignorant of Aboriginal culture and its considerable achievements, and its prejudice against them is ingrained. When major steps are taken in the education systems to combat this ignorance and prejudice, it is possible that the social climate could change to one of increased tolerance of the Aboriginal minority.[4]

Jigalong is far removed from all this ferment, yet the survival of the Aborigines' cultural heritage there depends ultimately on the willingness of white Australians to accept such diversity within their society. Tolerance of ethnic and cultural differences has never really been an Australian forte, despite the popularity of the ethic of "rugged individualism."[5] Well into the 1960s, the official government policy of assimilation as the goal of Aboriginal welfare programs was still operating, and it reflected a general disinclination of white Australians to accept cultural differences as a permanent feature of the society. "Assimilation" implied that Aborigines must eventually become culturally like the whites, regardless of whatever desires the Aborigines themselves might express with respect to their future in Australia.[6]

---

[3] Paul Coe, a leader of the Australian Aboriginal Black Power Movement, and currently a student in law at the University of New South Wales, participated in a symposium on Anthropology and Anti-Imperialism at the 1972 annual meeting of the American Anthropological Assiciation. He spoke on the treatment of Australian Aborigines and the growth of the Black Power movement, which is pressing for Aboriginal land rights and the creation of economically self-sufficient Aboriginal communities.

[4] This vitally important need for the education of white Australians in the nature of Aboriginal culture is discussed in a recent paper (Tonkinson 1971).

[5] For a readable and perceptive overview of contemporary white Australian culture, see Horne (1964).

[6] To quote an official definition: "The policy of assimilation means in the view of all Australian governments that all aborigines and part-aborigines are expected eventually to attain the same manner of living as other Australians and to live as members of a single Australian community enjoying the same responsibilities, observing the same customs and influenced by the same beliefs, hopes and loyalties as other Australians." (From "One People," prepared under the authority of the Minister for Territories, with the cooperation of the Ministers responsible for Aboriginal welfare in the Australian States, 1961).

With the recent change in federal government, a new and promising chapter is unfolding in the struggle for Aboriginal rights. One of the election platforms of the Labor Party, which came to power at the end of 1972, concerned the establishment of Aboriginal land rights, and steps have already been taken with a view to implementing the return of land to the Aborigines. The new policies suggest that the Aborigines may yet have some say in the role they will play in Australian society. Officialdom may now be more capable of accepting some form of integration as a possibility for Aboriginal groups that have managed to retain some of their traditional culture.[7] If the Australian public, too, could be induced to accept cultural pluralism as a workable possibility, and if this leads to the deliberate encouragement of Aborigines to maintain their identity, tradition-oriented communities in fairly isolated areas such as Jigalong could continue to exist for some time in the future.

For the attainment of long term and relatively successful integration, however, Aborigines would need the opportunity to increase their current socioeconomic status to a level commensurate with that of the bulk of the society. At present, the Aborigines are in all respects held at the bottom of the ladder. Unfortunately, employment opportunities in the drier interior of the continent are very limited and will probably remain so. In spite of their technological superiority, the whites have not been able to exploit the desert to their permanent advantage. Unlike the Aborigines in precontact days, they cannot sustain themselves there without considerable outside support. The Aborigines in settlements have lost many of their old skills and have become increasingly dependent on whites, to the extent that welfare payments are now a major source of sustenance. It is hardly necessary to point out the long term negative consequences of this situation, yet it appears to be an inevitable result of the current lack of employment opportunities.

In February 1973 the Minister for Aboriginal Affairs in the new government announced a grant of almost three million dollars

---

[7] Because the use of the term "integration" in the United States has generally meant "assimilation" and is therefore strongly objected to by U.S. Black Nationalists and other minorities, I should clarify my use of it. "Integration" as used here connotes a combination of cultural pluralism and socioeconomic equality.

($4.2 million in United States dollars) to Western Australia for Aboriginal advancement projects. He also noted that part of this grant would go to the Jigalong area in an effort to put effective control of the area in the hands of the Aborigines and to help them become socially and economically independent. It thus seems that major changes will soon be taking place in the Jigalong area, and the survival of the Law will depend very heavily on the way in which these changes are implemented and the extent to which the Aborigines are permitted to make decisions as to what they want to retain from the past.[8] Whatever else happens, the infusion of large sums of money into a long neglected marginal community will have profound consequences for its members and will produce changes that the Aborigines cannot possibly visualize at this stage of their acculturation.

If the history of culture contact in Australia is taken into account, it appears that the likelihood of any Aboriginal group integrating into the wider society, in such a way that it has economic viability yet retains much of its traditional values and behaviors, is remote. This is true even of Jigalong where the adaptation of the Aborigines has so far been markedly successful. As Gould notes:

> If developments continue as they have for the last 100 years, a success-
> ful and self-sustaining 10,000 year-old adaptation to the rigorous
> Western Desert environment will soon be replaced by two relatively
> unsuccessful and unstable adaptations; that of European-derived culture
> and that of the Europeanized culture of the Aborigines (1972:22).

Gould is writing of the southern and eastern parts of the Western Desert where the breakdown of traditional Aboriginal culture is noticeably greater and more rapid than at Jigalong, yet there is a certain inevitability in the general process of change. The forces of disintegration eventually triumph and Aboriginal society without its Law seems incapable of reintegrating in such a way that a satisfactory new equilibrium is reached. At Jigalong the Aborigines have triumphed over the agents of Apostolic Christianity and

---

[8] For any chance of success, it is essential that most decision-making power remain in the hands of the local Aborigines. In the United States, multi-million dollar grants to the poor and deprived have frequently resulted in economic prosperity for middle-class professional do-gooders (including, on occasion, social scientists) rather than the people for whose betterment the program was designed.

have rebuffed attempts by other Aboriginal groups to persuade them to compromise their Law. In view of the latest planned development, only time will tell if this can be any more than a holding action.

Bibliography

Ashley-Montagu, M. F.
    1937   *Coming into Being Among the Australian Aborigines.* London: Routledge.

Barnett, Homer G.
    1953   *Innovation: The Basis of Cultural Change.* New York: McGraw-Hill.

Bates, Daisy
    1938   *The Passing of the Aborigines.* London: Murray.

Berndt, Catherine H.
    1965   "Women and the 'Secret Life'," in *Aboriginal Man in Australia* (ed. R. and C. Berndt) pp. 238-282. Sydney: Angus and Robertson.

Berndt, Ronald M.
    1957   "Social and Cultural Change in Aboriginal Australia." *Proceedings of the Third Pan Indian Ocean Science Congress,* Section E., Tananarive.
    1959   "The Concept of 'The Tribe' in the Western Desert of Australia," *Oceania* 30:2:81-107.
    1963   "Groups with Minimal European Associations," in *Australian Aboriginal Studies* (ed. H. Shiels) pp. 385-408. Melbourne: Oxford.
    1970   "Traditional Morality as Expressed Through the Medium of an Australian Aboriginal Religion," in *Australian Aboriginal Anthropology* (ed. R. Berndt) pp. 216-247. Perth: University of Western Australia Press.

Berndt, R. and C.
    1945   "A Preliminary Report of Field Work in the Ooldea Region, Western South Australia," *Oceania Bound Offprint.* Sydney.
    1964   *The World of the First Australians.* Sydney: Ure Smith.
    1970   "Some Points of Change in Western Australia," in *Diprotodon to Detribalization* (ed. A. R. Pilling and R. A. Waterman) pp. 53-79. East Lansing: Michigan State University Press.

Broom, L. and P. Selznick
    1958   *Sociology.* New York: Row Peterson.

Burridge, K. O. L.
    1969   *New Heaven, New Earth.* Oxford: Blackwell.

Capell, A.
    1959   "Interpreting Christianity to Australian Aborigines," *The International Review of Missions* 38:1-11.

Cawte, J. E., Nari Djagamara and M. G. Barrett
    1966   "The meaning of subincision of the urethra to aboriginal Australians," *British Journal of Medical Psychology* 39:245-253.

Coon, Carleton S.
    1971   *The Hunting Peoples.* Boston: Atlantic-Little, Brown.

Douglas, W. H.
    1958   "An Introduction to the Western Desert Language of Australia," *Oceania Linguistic Monograph No. 4.* Sydney.

Elkin, A. P.
    1945   *Aboriginal Men of High Degree.* Sydney: Australasian Publishing Company.
    1951   "Reaction and Interaction: A Food Gathering People and European Settlement in Australia," *American Anthropologist* 53:164-186.
    1954   *The Australian Aborigines.* Sydney: Angus and Robertson.

Fink, Ruth A.
    n.d.   "A Mission that Fostered Tribal Custom," Australian School of Pacific Administration. (mimeographed).

Foster, George M.
    1962   *Traditional Cultures: and the Impact of Technological Change.* New York: Harper and Row.

Goodenough, Ward Hunt
    1963   *Cooperation in Change.* New York: Russell Sage Foundation.

Gould, Richard A.
    1967   "Notes on Hunting, Butchering, and Sharing of Game Among the Ngatatjara and their Neighbors in the Western Australian Desert," *Kroeber Anthropological Society Papers* 36:41-66.
    1968   "Living Archaeology: The Ngatatjara of Western Australia," *Southwestern Journal of Anthropology* 24:2:101-122.
    1969a *Yiwara: Foragers of the Australian Desert.* New York: Scribners.
    1969b "Subsistence Behavior Among the Western Desert Aborigines of Australia," *Oceania* 39:4:253-274.
    1970a "Spears and Spear-Throwers of the Western Desert Aborigines of Australia," *American Museum Novitates* 2403.
    1970b "Journey to Pulykara," *Natural History* 79:10:56-67.
    1971   "The archaeologist as ethnographer: a case from the Western Desert of Australia," *World Archaeology* 3:2:143-177.
    1972   "Progress to Oblivion," *The Ecologist* 2:9:17-22.

Herald of Grace
    1963   "Let's Go to Jigalong," *Herald of Grace* 22:2:30-33.

Hiatt, L. R.
    1962   "Local Organization among the Australian Aborigines," *Oceania* 32:4:267-286.
    1966   "The lost horde," *Oceania* 37:2:81-92.

Horne, Donald
    1964   *The Lucky Country: Australia in the Sixties.* Baltimore: Penguin.

Jones, F. Lancaster
    1970   *The Structure and Growth of Australia's Aboriginal Population.* Canberra: Australian National University Press.

Kaberry, Phyllis M.
    1939   *Aboriginal Woman, Sacred and Profane.* London: Routledge.

Kirk, R. L.
    1971   "Genetic Evidence and its Implications for Aboriginal Pre-history," in *Aboriginal Man and Environment in Australia* (ed. D. J. Mulvaney and J. Golson) pp. 326-343. Canberra: Australian National University Press.

Lee, R. B. and I. DeVore (ed.)
    1968   *Man the Hunter.* Chigaco: Aldine.

Lévi-Strauss, Claude
    1963   *Totemism* (R. Needham, trans.). Boston: Beacon.

Lindgren, Eric
    1961   "Natural History Notes from Jigalong, North-Western
           Australia," *The West Australian Naturalist* 7:5:122-128.

Linton, Ralph
    1955   *The Tree of Culture.* New York: Knopf.

Long, J. P. M.
    1964a   "Papunya: Westernization in an Aboriginal Community," in
           Aborigines Now (ed. M. Reay) pp. 72-82. Sydney: Angus and
           Robertson.
    1964b   "The Pintubi Patrols: Welfare Work with Desert Aborigines,"
           Australian Territories 4:5:43-48; 4:6:24-35.
    1971   "Arid Region Aborigines: The Pintubi," in *Aboriginal Man and
           Environment in Australia* (ed. D. J. Mulvaney and J. Golson)
           pp. 262-270. Canberra: Australian National University Press.

Meggitt, M. J.
    1962   *Desert People.* Sydney: Angus and Robertson.
    1965   "The Association between Australian Aborigines and Dingoes,"
           in *Man, culture and animals: the role of animals in human
           ecological adjustments* (ed. A. Leeds and A. P. Vayda) pp. 7-26.
           Washington, D. C.: American Association for the Advancement
           of Science.
    1966   "Gadjari Among the Walbiri Aborigines of Central Australia,"
           Oceania Monograph No. 14. Sydney.

Merton, Robert K.
    1957   *Social Theory and Social Structure.* Glencoe: Free Press.

Moorehead, Alan
    1967   *The Fatal Impact.* New York: Dell.

Mountford, C. P.
    1937-9 "Aboriginal Crayon Drawings from the Warburton Ranges in
           Western Australia," *Transactions of the Royal Society of South
           Australia* 61-63.

Mountford, C. P. and Robert Tonkinson
    1969   "Carved and Engraved Human Figures from North Western Australia," *Anthropological Forum* 2:3:371-390.

Munn, Nancy D.
    1965   "A Report on Field Research at Areyonga (1964-1965)," *Australian Institute of Aboriginal Studies* (mimeographed). Canberra.
    1970   "The Transformation of Subjects into Objects in Walbiri and Pitjantjatjara Myth," in *Australian Aboriginal Anthropology* (ed. R. M. Berndt) pp. 141-163. Perth: University of Western Australia Press.
    1973   *Walbiri Iconography*. Ithaca: Cornell University Press.

Radcliffe-Brown, A. R.
    1930-1 "The Social Organization of Australian Tribes," *Oceania* 1-4.
    1952   *Structure and Function in Primitive Society*. London: Cohen and West.

Rowley, C. D.
    1970   *The Destruction of Aboriginal Society*. Canberra: Australian National University Press.

Sahlins, Marshall
    1972   *Stone Age Economics*. Chicago: Aldine.

Schusky, Ernest L.
    1972   *Manual for Kinship Analysis*. (Second Edition). New York: Holt, Rinehart and Winston.

Spencer, B. and F.J. Gillen
    1938   *The Native Tribes of Central Australia*. London: Macmillan.

Stanner, W. E. H.
    1958   "The Dreaming," in *Reader in Comparative Religion* (ed. W.A. Lessa and E. Z. Vogt) pp. 513-523. New York: Harper and Row.
    1965a "Religion, Totemism and Symbolism," in *Aboriginal Man in Australia* (ed. R. M. and C. H. Berndt) pp. 207-237. Sydney: Angus and Robertson.
    1965b "Aboriginal territorial organization: estate, range, domain and regime," *Oceania* 36:1:1-26.
    1966   "On Aboriginal Religion," *Oceania Monograph No. 11*. Sydney.

Strehlow, T. G. H.
1947   *Aranda Traditions.* Melbourne: Melbourne University Press.
1965   "Culture, Social Structure and Environment in Aboriginal
        Central Australia," in *Aboriginal Man in Australia* (ed. R. M.
        and C. H. Berndt) pp. 121-145. Sydney: Angus and Robertson.
1970   "Geography and the Totemic Landscape in Central Australia:
        A Functional Study," in *Australian Aboriginal Anthropology*
        (ed. R. M. Berndt) pp. 92-140. Perth: University of Western
        Australia Press.

Tindale, Norman E.
1936   "Legend of the Wati Kutjara, Warburton Range, Western Aus-
        tralia," *Oceania* 7:2:169-185.

Tonkinson, Robert
1966   "Social Structure and Acculturation of Aborigines in the
        Western Desert," Unpublished M. A. thesis. University of
        Western Australia.
1970   "Aboriginal Dream-Spirit Beliefs in a Contact Situation: Jiga-
        long, Western Australia," in *Australian Aboriginal Anthropology*
        (ed. R. M. Berndt) pp. 277-291. Perth: University of Western
        Australia Press.
1971   "Towards the Education of White Australians," *Origin* 5:3:4.
1972   "Ŋa:wajil: A Western Desert Aboriginal Rainmaking Ritual,"
        Unpublished Ph.D. thesis. University of British Columbia.

Warner, W. Lloyd
1937/64 *A Black Civilization.* New York: Harper.

Wells, L. A.
1902   *Journal of the Calvert Scientific Exploring Expedition, 1896-7.*
        Perth: Government Printer.

Wilson, John
1961   "Authority and Leadership in a 'New Style' Australian Aborig-
        inal Community, Pindan, Western Australia," Unpublished M. A.
        thesis. University of Western Australia.

Wilson, Katrin
1961   "The Allocation of Sex Roles in Social and Economic Affairs
        in a 'New Style' Australian Aboriginal Community, Pindan,
        Western Australia," Unpublished M. Sc. thesis. University of
        Western Australia.

Wilson, Katrin
   1970   "Pindan: A Preliminary Comment," in *Diprotodon to Detrib-*
          alization (ed. A. R. Pilling and R. A. Waterman) pp. 333-346.
          East Lansing: Michigan State University Press.

Wolcott, Harry F.
   1972   "Too True to be Good: The Subculture of American Mission-
          aries in Urban Africa," *Practical Anthropology* 19:6:241-258.

Worsley, Peter M.
   1967   "Groote Eylandt Totemism and Le Totémisme aujourd'hui,"
          in *The Structural Study of Myth and Totemism* (ed. Edmund
          Leach) pp. 141-159. London: Tavistock.

Yengoyan, Aram
   1970   "Demographic Factors in Pitjandjara Social Organization," in
          Australian Aboriginal Anthropology (ed. R. M. Berndt) pp. 70-
          91. Perth: University of Western Australia Press.

Index